MICROCOSM PUBLISHING is Portland's most diversified publishing house and distributor, with a focus on the colorful, authentic, and empowering. Our books and zines have put your power in your hands since 1996, equipping readers to make positive changes in their lives and in the world around them. Microcosm emphasizes skill-building, showing hidden histories, and fostering creativity through challenging conventional publishing wisdom with books and bookettes about DIY skills, food, bicycling, gender, self-care, and social justice. What was once a distro and record label started by Joe Biel in a drafty bedroom was determined to be *Publishers Weekly*'s fastest-growing publisher of 2022 and #3 in 2023, and is now among the oldest independent publishing houses in Portland, OR, and Cleveland, OH. We are a politically moderate, centrist publisher in a world that has inched to the right for the past 80 years.

Global labor conditions are bad, and our roots in industrial Cleveland in the '70s and '80s made us appreciate the need to treat workers right. Therefore, our books are MADE IN THE USA.

Queer HORROR

Fun & Freaky Perspectives on Macabre Media

Gina Brandolino
& Joe Carlough

MICROCOSM PUBLISHING
Portland, Ore | Cleveland, Ohio

QUEER HORROR
Fun & Freaky Perspectives on Macabre Media

First edition - 2,000 copies - July 1, 2025
ISBN 9781648415111
This is Microcosm # 959
Edited by Lex Orgera
Cover by Lindsey Cleworth
Design by Joe Biel

To join the ranks of high-class stores that feature Microcosm titles, talk to your rep: In the U.S. **COMO** (Atlantic), **ABRAHAM** (Midwest), **BOB BARNETT** (Texas, Oklahoma, Arkansas, Louisiana), **IMPRINT** (Pacific), **TURNAROUND** (UK and Europe), **UTP/MANDA** (Canada), **NEWSOUTH** (Australia/New Zealand), **Observatoire** (Africa, Europe), **IPR** (Middle East), **APD** (Asia), **HarperCollins** (India), and **FAIRE** in the gift trade.

For a catalog, write or visit:
Microcosm Publishing
2752 N Williams Ave.
Portland, OR 97227
All the news that's fit to print at www.Microcosm.Pub/Newsletter

Get more copies of this book at www.Microcosm.Pub/QueerHorror

Did you know that you can buy our books directly from us at sliding scale rates? Support a small, independent publisher and pay less than Amazon's price at **www.Microcosm.Pub.**

EU Safety Information: https://microcosmpublishing.com/gpsr

Library of Congress Cataloging-in-Publication Data
Names: Brandolino, Gina author | Carlough, Joseph author
Title: Queer horror : fun and freaky perspectives on macabre media / by Gina Brandolino, Joe Carlough.
Description: Portland, OR : Microcosm Publishing, 2025. | Includes index. |Summary: "Don't be scared straight! Curl up on the couch with Joe and Gina for a romp through their favorite horror movies, TV shows, and books from the 1930s to today, exploring their messages, meaning, and enduring appeal for queer audiences"— Provided by publisher.
Identifiers: LCCN 2025024905 | ISBN 9781648415111 paperback
Classification: LCC PN1995.9.H6 B636 2025 | DDC 791.43/6164—dc23/eng/20250530
LC record available at https://lccn.loc.gov/2025024905

CONTENTS

THIS IS THE HORROR WE KNEW WHEN WE WERE KIDS

A General Introduction to Our Book

When we started our zine series, *Gina and Joe Talk About*, we didn't intend to create a series that focused solely on queer horror. The first issue was about *Queer Horror*, sure, written so we would have our first zine ready in time for Pride 2021. That zine will always hold a special place in our hearts: it was our first project together, and we used it to delve deeper into our motivations for loving horror and what it has meant to us and our identities, a theme that runs through the entirety of this book! We followed that issue with issues on *Halloween Horror*, *Wintry Horrors*, *Queer Horror II*, and in 2023, in honor of the classic movie's fiftieth anniversary, *The Exorcist*. We weren't planning to make most of our critical essays on horror *intentionally* about queerness if that wasn't important to our theses.

But we *are* queer people, which will forever influence how we see and digest horror. And while a lot of these essays deal explicitly with queerness and our own journeys, some come from a place of our own love of horror, and how we watch horror films and read horror stories. Gina's an out lesbian who met her spouse Ellen twenty-five years ago when they were both in graduate school. Joe's a more-recently out bisexual who finally learned to embrace his queer experiences—and himself. We set out to write essays about the genre of horror *as* queer people. These identities will forever influence how we take in any media, and it turns out horror has a lot to say about the queer experience, and we have a lot to add to that discussion ourselves, whether we're connecting a particular genre to our queer identities, relating personal anecdotes to our favorite movies, or digging into what we love about the horror genre outside of what it is to be a queer horror fan.

As we were soon to find out, it can be hard to write any essay and not have our identities influence our take on the genre. Any discussion of nature vs. nurture, whether we are who we are because of some intrinsic us-ness vs. the environment we were raised in, usually ends with the same sentiment: *it's both, dummy.* In Joe's essay "They're Coming For You, Barbra," he draws parallels between discovering and then accepting his queerness through his love of horror (and a little talk therapy). It's an essay about external stimuli—horror movies, everyday interactions, childhood relationships—and how they directly brought him down the path to exploring his own identity as it relates to sexuality, gender, and presentation. But none of that *made* him gay: instead, it fostered a little whisper that continued to grow louder. Once he understood how to listen, that is.

Gina's essay "Summer of Dread" delicately threads the needle of life experience. In it, she describes moving as a child from her hometown of Joliet, Illinois, where her house was "not three miles away from Stateville Prison," to a more rural area, the kind of place her partner Ellen would later say she feels safe due to the lack of bad guys, but a place where both child *and* adult Gina feel "a pronounced lack of people to help if you get in a jam." Being far from the comfort of a nearby neighbor or an easy explanation for the noise outside the window was a source of constant unease for young Gina. The anxiety she felt as a little girl, the dread, the feeling of *should we even be outside of the house right now?* are the feelings any horror fan—and, sadly, queer person—can relate to. At least in a city you can usually *find your people*, your found family, but it can be hard to do so when there aren't that many people to start with!

We're not trying to say everyone who felt anxiety as a child is gay—let's face it, if that were the case, we'd all be *super* gay. What we're saying is that the experiences we all have in childhood help to shape us. Every feeling of fear, every time we feel unsafe, is a lesson learned. And as queer people, we learn a lot of lessons that heteronormative people might never have to even consider.

At the end of the day, horror is what has brought us together, in this book. We wouldn't have even met if not for our joint love of horror: Gina wrote to Joe after reading a series of Victorian and early 1900s horror stories he'd re-published as zines, and it was shortly after that the idea of our zine series was born. Put any two horror fans in the same room and they'll have much to discuss, regardless of what they love about the genre: one may love big budget horror while the other loves homemade scary movies; one may love slashers while the other loves ghost stories; heck, one might fastidiously curate a list of the over five hundred horror movies they've recently seen on their computer (*::cough, JOE, cough::*) and the other might be constantly reading, listening to, and watching horror to find new material for the courses she teaches on horror (*aka Gina's roving syllabus eye*). Those two people will still most likely have an animated conversation about horror and, more importantly, how they *feel* when they watch a scary movie. It brought Gina and Joe together, and look, it's working again, because here we are, in conversation with you as you read our book.

In our experience as avid horror fans, there's no shortage of conversation to be had around horror and how it makes us feel. Some of the essays included see us discussing our gender and sexuality, like when Joe explores using movie characters to try on different identities in his essay "Genderplay at the World's Fair"; some show us sounding the depths of our own fear, like Gina talks about in her essay "Lost Girls"; and some see us just being scared, or enjoying a particular piece of media and sharing our joy—queer or otherwise!

One of the aspects of the horror genre that is always surprising to us is the grand range of responses any number of people can have to the same movie. In the scheme of personal critique, the essays included in this book are our responses to some movies, books, and poems you may have seen and, hopefully, a few you haven't. It's our recommendation that you experience the stories we discuss on your own before reading the essays about them if you don't have a comfortable recollection of them or don't want spoilers. We want this book to be a conversation between a few horror fans, whether you're keeping that database like Joe or dreaming of lesson plans for your students like Gina, or anywhere in between.

With Love & Horror,

Gina & Joe

THE FINAL GIRL IS ALL OF US

Personal Introductions

Monsters and Final Girls

GINA

In the fall of 2017, I walked into a tattoo shop toting a big slab of a book, Emil Ferris's graphic novel *My Favorite Thing Is Monsters, Book I.* I had a bunch of different pages marked that offered different views of the story's protagonist, Karen Reyes. Karen is a ten-year-old girl growing up in what no one would call an affluent neighborhood in Chicago in the late 1960s. At home, she's got an eccentric mother and a tough older brother, both of whom truly adore her. But she's also got a secret: She likes girls. She doesn't really know how to act on these feelings, but nonetheless she can sense the ways they alienate her at school and even at home, and that's with her keeping it mostly to herself. She knows that if she were more open about how she feels about other girls, it would single her out in every context she inhabits. That makes her day-to-day life pretty uncomfortable, but she's found a way to cope. She loves horror stories of all kinds, any way she can get them—late night TV movie features, comic books, pulp magazines. She loves them especially for their monsters, whom she sees as misunderstood, wrongly shunned and vilified, and alienated in ways that she deeply understands. More than sympathizing with them, she identifies with them. She's not just the book's protagonist, but also its narrator; the story unfolds in words and pictures set down in her private notebook. And she draws herself as the most adorable little werewolf you've ever seen.

Karen Reyes hit me hard when I first read *My Favorite Thing Is Monsters*, and she hits me as hard with every re-reading. I grew up more or less in her era (she was ten in the late 1960s; I was born in 1972), and more or less in her area (she grew up in Chicago; I grew up in the south suburbs). I didn't have her clarity of preference for romantic partners when I was ten years old, but I was definitely aware that I wasn't an ordinary little girl. Like her, I didn't fit in so well at school. Like her, even though I was truly loved at home and had friends, I often felt my difference from them, which made me feel disconnected, isolated. I *get* Karen Reyes; she speaks to my soul. I wanted her tattooed on my arm too, partly to celebrate her, partly to protect her. That might sound weird, but I know the feelings Karen has when other characters look askance at her in *My Favorite Thing Is Monsters*; I remember the feelings I had when it happened to me as a kid. Now that I'm older, when people look askance at me, I don't feel small and scared anymore. I don't really expect people to come up to me, point at my tattoo, and ask with derision, "What's with the werewolf girl on your arm?!" But I sure dare them to.

After I showed the tattoo artist *My Favorite Thing Is Monsters*, we talked and sketched out ideas for my tattoo. As we did, the book sort of spontaneously got passed around among the six or eight other people in the shop—other artists, other customers, mostly (or all) women, and mostly (or all) queer. I have said that Karen Reyes is an adorable werewolf, but I don't think everyone in the world would share my opinion on that. She's still a monster, after all: she has fangs with a wicked underbite, is a bit furry, and has pointy, animal-like ears. Even beyond her more stereotypical monstrous attributes, she does her hair in a sort of pompadour, has ochre-colored skin, and prefers to dress androgynously. As the book made the rounds, I got anxious, my protective instincts flaring. Were these people going to make fun of Karen? But they didn't! They *ooohed* and *aaahed* over her: they, too, thought she was adorable, and super cool. One of them said, "This werewolf looks *really* familiar!" Others expressed agreement. I piped up: "Of course she does! She's all of us!" In that shop, we all knew something about what it was like to be Karen Reyes.

Queer people know what it's like to be othered, seen as different, vile, dangerous; to be scorned, dreaded, rejected in ways subtle and gross. And just as Karen Reyes seemed familiar to everyone in that tattoo shop, the monster often seems familiar to queer folks. Take Frankenstein's monster—admittedly the most pathetic of antagonists, so full of heart and so misunderstood that, well, wait, *are you sure he's a monster?* His anger and frustration towards the characters who judge and reject him because his body looks so different from other bodies make sense to queer audiences. He inspired trans scholar Susan Stryker to write "My Words to Victor Frankenstein Above the Village of Chamounix: Performing Transgender Rage," a powerful essay published in *A Journal of Gay and Lesbian Studies.* But what about other monsters with less pathos, with aims and goals less legible to us, with means more violent and sinister? Like, say, Freddy Krueger? In his article "'There's Something Inside of Me': Coming Out as a Gay Horror Fan," Louis Pietzman writes about being a closeted gay teenager encountering Freddy: "What scared me more than his burned face and knife-fingers were his winks and sass. He was so out there—and it looked like he was having fun." Pietzman was scared by—and also drawn to—Freddy's gay edge, and he isn't alone. More than a few queer horror fans find a kindred spirit in Freddy, see his fearless, in-your-face attitude as a liberating alternative to being ashamed and afraid of how people will react to you. A whole queer subculture has grown up around the *A Nightmare on Elm Street* series; you can watch the documentary *Scream, Queen!* to learn more about it. And let's not forget the Babadook, the monster from the 2014 movie of the same name that features a little creature who feeds off trauma and grief—and causes more of both. While there's nothing explicit in the movie that signals queer themes, after a Tumblr poster proposed it, queer fans of the movie were quick to claim this despised, feared monster who is barely acknowledged except to be repulsed by those he shares a house with; they knew how he felt. This interpretation of the Babadook grew like wildfire, and now it's canon: The Babadook is one of us.

Look, I'm not saying that killing off the entire family line of your enemy (that's Frankenstein's monster), being a child murderer (Freddy Krueger), or terrorizing grief-stricken families (the Babadook) is okay. But those aren't the monstrous qualities queer folks identify with in these stories. Frankenstein's monster looks different, Freddy isn't appropriately masculine, and the Babadook is trying to make a home where he isn't wanted. It's hardly a surprise that characters with these qualities are identified as monsters in stories; and because we've often been judged by similar (or, indeed, *exactly the same*) measures, it's also hardly a surprise that queer people identify with them. Like Karen Reyes, we have a sort of insider perspective on what it's like to be them; we have access to different stories than the ones that get explicitly told about them. Like Karen does with the monsters she loves, we see the ways they're misunderstood, wrongly shunned and vilified, and alienated. We see ourselves in these monsters.

But however much I adore Karen Reyes—and it's *a lotttt*—I don't think that, when it comes to horror stories, it's just the monster, always the monster, with whom queer people can or do identify. That's not our only option. I think we can often also see ourselves in the hero, and one particular kind of hero especially: We're all such resilient final girls! If you're into horror you might know this term, coined by Carol Clover in her influential book *Men, Women, and Chainsaws: Gender in the Modern Horror Film.* The final girl is the one left standing when the dust settles at the end of a story: the one who kills the monster, or at least gets away from it and leaves it frustrated. She lives to tell the tale.

The final girl of modern horror movies owes a debt to the girls in those shopworn but never obsolete urban legends: the hook, the babysitter and the killer upstairs, the killer in the backseat. But in these stories, usually, there is *no* final girl—the killer gets them all. As Jan Harold Brunvand explains in his book *The Vanishing Hitchhiker: American Urban Legends and Their Meanings,* the horror in these stories does more than entertain us; along the way, it reinforces incredibly traditional, even suffocating, social and cultural values. The female characters who die in these stories are punished for doing something "wrong": they're at college when they should be married, not pursuing a career; out on dates experimenting with sex; or babysitting, sure—but are they really watching the baby that closely if a killer has gotten to them? If these "infractions" seem to you like slim justification for gruesome death at the hands of a crazed killer, you're not wrong. In his book *Danse Macabre,* Stephen King suggests that many horror stories are "as conservative as an Illinois Republican in a three-piece pinstriped suit," and that often, their "main purpose is to reaffirm the virtues of the norm by showing us what awful things happen to people who venture into taboo lands." Urban legends are good examples of the horror stories King has in mind here. It turns out horror has more than monsters like the ones with whom Karen Reyes identifies, more than just monsters who know what it's like to be queer. There are socially conservative monsters out there, too—but final girls get the better of them.

The list of final girls is long, badass, and growing all the time (and increasingly, not filled with just the names of female characters—Chris Washington in *Get Out*, for example, fits the final girl mold). To name a few of the founding badasses from the golden era of the final girl, the 1970s: Sally Hardesty of *The Texas Chainsaw Massacre* (1974), a girl reckless enough to leave hearth and home to take a road trip with her brother and friends, who lolsobs at the thwarted killer, Leatherface, from the back of the pickup truck she escapes in while he chops the air with his chainsaw in frustration. Jess from the little-known but excellent Canadian Christmas horror classic *Black Christmas* (1974), who was haughty enough to stay at her sorority house over the Christmas holiday rather than go home to celebrate with her family, outsmarts a killer picking off her sorority sisters one by one. Laurie Strode of *Halloween* (1978) is the later incarnation of that babysitter in the urban legend about the babysitter and the killer upstairs, only she saves the kid she's watching and also faces down the inscrutable Michael Myers using her wits and a ton of nerve. None of these girls does anything they deserve to be punished for; they've just managed to run afoul of psychopaths with really benighted ideas about where girls should and shouldn't be, and what girls should and shouldn't be allowed to do. And these final girls *do not back down*; they don't apologize, rethink their choices, or "learn their place." They say *hell no* and fight back. And they win!

So, does any of that sound familiar? Do you know anyone who has people with conservative values, an over-inflated sense of the importance of their opinions, and a lot of power (not to mention potentially violent power) trying to tell them what they can and can't do? The final girl is *all of us*. She represents anyone who has stood up against that nasty species of socially conservative monster. She's anyone who kept holding hands with their partner when they noticed the glares and snarls of the people around them, who called out the homophobic slur rather than let it pass, who took the punch standing rather than run away when the gay bar was overrun. And more.

Karen Reyes's favorite thing is without a doubt monsters, but even at the tender age of ten, she's getting lessons in how to embrace her inner final girl, too. Karen's coming of age as a queer person isn't the whole story of *My Favorite Thing Is Monsters*, over even the biggest story—and the story got bigger when *Book II* came out in spring of 2024. At the heart of the plot of both books is the murder of Karen's beloved neighbor Anka, a German Jew who managed to survive World War II. Karen takes it upon herself to try to solve Anka's murder. As she investigates, she learns more than a little about the sex trade in Nazi Germany as well as the concentration camps and complicated decisions characters made to save themselves and others from them. All that's pretty heavy, but there's more. Karen's home life is increasingly messy and sad, seemingly everyone in her neighborhood is implicated somehow in the mafia, and the turbulent political events of the late 1960s shake her corner of Chicago no less than the rest of the country. It's a lot for a little werewolf to endure. And while her monster status—her queerness—isn't the lynchpin of each of these storylines, it's not incidental, either. What makes her feel different also gives her an unshakable sense of self, and it makes her brave. More than once or twice, she has to stand up against rudeness, hostility, and even threats of violence. She holds her ground; she's a tough little kid. For me, part of the invigorating joy of reading *My Favorite Thing Is Monsters* is seeing Karen take her first steps towards *hell no.* She is without question a badass in the making.

I've just made the case that monsters are both *us* and *them*—both queer folks who know what it is to be rebuked and reviled and the social conservatives who rebuke and revile us. Same with the protagonists of horror: I've said they're both *us,* the resilient and resourceful final girls, and *them,* the shallow-minded, scared characters who plot and plan against the monster. The richness of horror—and especially the way horror intersects with the queer experience—means that there are many different ways to see ourselves reflected in the genre and to use it to find our place in our own stories. Who says it has to be just one or the other? We're all monsters, and we're all final girls—*both and.* You, me, and Karen Reyes too.

Hi Everyone, It's Me, Barbra.

JOE

Hi everyone, it's me, Barbra. And they're coming for me. I see the ghouls shambling, but my brother Johnny doesn't believe me—even worse, he's taunting me about it. I'm about to live through the *Night of the Living Dead.*

I'm Angela in *Night of the Demons,* and I know a presence has just entered the room. I'm just *the weirdo from history class, a lonely old misfit trying to get attention.* I know something bad has just happened, I can see it in the faces of my friends, feel it in the wind that's just blown through our circle. But they're all too drunk, too stupid, or too horny to feel it.

Or, oh, I don't know, I could be any number of children seeing the monster slip out of the closet, the languid claw sliding out from under my bed, only to retreat back under when confronted by "an adult," any person who I feel holds real authority over my life.

At the end of the day, I'm just myself: a horror fan attempting to sort through my complicated feelings about gender, queerness, and femininity. Something terrifies me about being the disbelieved woman, the child who no one takes seriously. I'm scared of disharmony. I don't know if I have the language to speak critically about the phenomenon of the disbelieved woman in movies, but I certainly have the emotional connection to *being* disbelieved.

As of writing this book, it's been four years since Gina and I started our horror essay zine series, *Gina and Joe Talk About.* Our first issue was *Queer Horror*, a zine we enjoyed writing so much that we continued the series—for a total of five issues before this book! The zine really resonated with so many people, in part because of the excellent cover image: a piece of clipart I found in an old clip art pack of "100,000+ royalty free images for you to use!" titled "Fabulous Vampire Costume."

I used that zine as the vehicle to come out publicly, to be queer in places other than just my mind, my *Animal Crossing: New Horizons* island, my therapist's office, and long conversations with my wonderful partner, Katie, who also identifies as queer. I don't know if embracing my queerness publicly was much of a surprise to anyone, but because I did so, the past few years have been filled with queer experiences—exqueeriences?—that have been uplifting, life-altering, terrifying, and exhausting. They say you don't just come out once, that you come out over and over again. I feel like I've come out a hundred times since then.

In the middle of all this, I went to Iceland.

In 2022, Katie and I were awarded a writer's residency in the capital city of Reykjavík through Bókmenntaborgin, the Reykjavík UNESCO City of Literature program. We were to spend a little over a month living in the basement apartment of Gröndalshús, a historic-house-turned-museum that was originally occupied by naturalist and poet Benedikt Gröndal. We packed our bags, found someone to watch our house here in Philadelphia, and spent a month in my new favorite place, as the city's first-ever duo of writers to stay in the apartment.

There are a multitude of reasons why I loved my experience in Iceland: the gentleness of the culture, the widespread queer values, the deep-rooted respect for (and proliferation of!) art and literature, the incredible lack of violent crime. I felt at home there. I spent the month working on an issue of my music magazine, *Hit the Decks,* writing my first book for Microcosm, *The Queer Affirmations Coloring Book,* and watching Icelandic horror movies, many of which you can read about later in this book. In Reykjavík, K & I worked all morning and walked all afternoon—finding geothermal footbaths among the rocks on the beaches, meandering through majestic landscapes, and patting more friendly cats than you could shake a stick at. We spent many nights in a queer metal bar called Gaukurinn. I even donated a copy of the first issue of the zine *Queer Horror* to the city library, Borgarbókasafnið Grófinni, where the librarian—who was wearing a rainbow lanyard, I might add—promised they'd display it among other books during Pride month. It felt good to be not only accepted in my burgeoning identity, but also a part of the celebration.

It was a hard landing, coming back home. To the country that had just repealed *Roe v. Wade.* To the city where I'm called a f*g in the streets at least a few times a year. To the casual violence of car horns, muggings, shouted expletives, carjackings, littered streets, shootings, *Make America Great Again* flags. To a drug epidemic so pervasive and intense that I see it on the news, in the streets downtown, at my train stations and bus stops, on the porch across the street from our house. I used to feel differently about all this. I was proud to live in a city that was so tough. I didn't think a life that I wanted could exist outside of this city, or any city like it; in order to live in a place that was otherwise full of the things I love, like art, music, and the kind of people I admire, I just had to put up with some shit. Or so I thought. I didn't really know there was a place that could be safe and gentle, refreshing and progressive, and still have so many of those things, still brimming with exciting, young art. I might be back at home in Philadelphia, but I'm afraid I might no longer *feel* at home in Philadelphia. I let down my guard in Iceland. I softened my ability to live in a tough place. I'm having a hard time building that wall back up. I feel afraid of my city, but even more importantly, I feel unsafe in my country.

Afraid. Fear is at the heart of all horror movies. Psychologists have probed the films and their fans, picking apart what makes horror such a popular genre. One idea that's gained some traction is that we find what we fear in movies and we face it there, which better prepares us to one day meet that fear in real life. When we watch a scary movie, the exhilaration of terror is followed by the warm feeling of safety, of nest-building. We scare ourselves so that our lives don't feel so scary. It's a reasonable explanation of the genre and one that I can apply pretty easily to my own love of horror: I challenge myself to accept hidden parts of myself, devouring allegorical ghost stories, relating to society through zombies and vampires, questioning inner demons—*are you evil or are you just a misunderstood part of me?* Horror is a place where I can probe my queerness, something I was once too scared to do otherwise.

I've always tended to go for haunted houses and monsters, movies that could be described by genre tags like *ghastly, ambient, spooky, supernatural,* or *zombie, gore, terror, creature feature.* I wanted monsters and ghosts, shadows in the corner. The heaviness of *Crimson Peak,* a quiet house when someone is alone. The shadow in the doorway of *The Dark and the Wicked.* Waking up to a soft footstep on the staircase, an item being knocked to the floor at the end of your bed, only to realize your partner, sibling, roommate, *whoever,* is still asleep. Stepping into a room in the moments after a verbal altercation, when the words hang low in the air and you can feel the hurt. If Katie was going to be out of the house for a night, I wanted to fill my night with really scary shit so I could go upstairs and hide under the covers alone, feel the fear of every creak and pop in our old house. It was exciting to be scared. But lately, I've begun to shift to a new genre, a genre I'm coining as something highly personalized, something I'm already collecting as a new go-to list for movies to watch again: Comfort Horror. What qualifies as "comforting" will differ from person to person, of course. For me, I'm drenching myself in kitschy eighties movies, which often establish a focus on the popular aesthetics and fashion of the time, like in *Chopping Mall* and *Prom Night 2: Hello Mary Lou.* I want the cheese and glitz of the early nineties, the impossible monsters in the sewers of New York City in *Mimic*, the chimera evolving in the museum basement in *Relic* who only emerges once the fancypants fundraising gala is in full swing. I want scary movies that *don't* scare me. I want to watch twenty-eight-year-olds playing teenagers being chased by ghouls and demons while decked out in the height of their decade's new fashion. I want the nostalgic rush of a cassette deck playing eerie music on its own and neon shoelaces that tie themselves together to trip up the heroine at a crucial moment. I want to watch *Amityville Horror* movies—but not the first few scary ones, the ones about ridiculous haunted clocks and anthropomorphic lamps bought at a yard sale.

Maybe all my life I've been feeling scared without realizing it, and now that I do realize it, I don't want to feel so scared anymore. I don't want the jolt to my system when someone knocks too aggressively on my door, or the guys on the porch across the street are having a conversation so loudly that I can hear every word, even with my windows closed: and, spoiler alert, they're not talking about nice things, they're not being kind to each other. I want to *choose* when I feel afraid, not have fear be such a part of my everyday experience. I've been thinking more and saying less. I'm probing what queerness could mean to me, after a solid thirty-something years of being a "straight guy" who often felt emotionally confused about his sense of self. I'm drawing lines between the way people have treated me throughout my life and the affinity I have towards the girlfriend in the movie, the daughter, the wife. I have a lot of work left to do on understanding what those drawn lines mean for me and mean for my sense of self moving forward, but when I allow myself to think about myself as a queer, feminine man, I feel like an old ghost has gotten off my chest, and I can breathe again. And I'm getting a lot better at saying what I mean, even when it's hard for me to say or hard for someone to hear. I'm feeling a lot better for it, and perhaps more importantly, a lot more "believed."

For decades, horror has provided me with a way to explore some of my deep, inner workings, without actually having to face them—a kind of unguided therapy before I ever experienced talk therapy. This often happened regardless of the intended message of the movie. Like, how do I relate to Angela's gender in *Sleepaway Camp*? As a kid I really took that in. *Sometimes I feel like I'm both a boy and a girl; could that be me?* Am I a member of Vincent Price's *Monster Club*, an outcast freak who's found a home in a dark alley punk club in London? Is it meaningful that I find it so deliciously satisfying when protagonist Billy shoots the homophobic cop in *Butcher, Baker, Nightmare Maker?* I watched those movies, completely aware of some of the messages they were *intending* to convey but looking past those messages for my own, secret meanings. I might have formally come out the summer of 2021, but I'd probably come out much earlier through horror movies; I just didn't know how to interpret it as such.

I *am* lucky, though, to have those safer spaces. To have my comfortable house, with a partner I love and all my family and friends on speed dial. To have my creative projects and all my collaborators who want to talk about their lives with me, with whom I get to share special moments and create great pieces of art. I'm really lucky to have Gina, someone who loves horror just as much as I do and who wants to dig into her love of the genre with me. And I can be nice to myself in other ways: Katie & I are finding a few more excuses to get to Iceland when we can. We have some friends there now who I'm beginning to consider good friends—people I talk to from afar even if we can't see each other often (Hi, Íris!).

I might not always feel at home in my physical location, but I can feel at home with people like you, the reader of this book. We can create a home together, you and I, coming together to explore what we love about horror movies and what it is about being queer that brings horror to the forefront. Is it finding the monster in ourselves? Finding ourselves in the monster? Probably a bit of both. And probably a lot of other things, too. In the pages of this book, I'm going to revel in the nostalgic comfort of the eighties and early nineties, my movie role models who, for decades, I didn't even know were role models. I'll imagine I'm in the theater with the college movie dorks in *Popcorn,* decorating for the horror festival in a montage set to reggae music. I'll be one of the punks in the van with Bettina Ciampolini in *Demons,* innocently enjoying a night of personal mayhem and depravity. I'll try to look nearly as good as Tawny Kitaen looks in *Witchboard.* Or as good as Kathleen Wilhoite looks in *Witchboard.* Why did everyone look so great in *Witchboard?*

So I might feel disbelieved like Barbra from *Night of the Living Dead* sometimes, but I don't have to. Maybe I'm Reggie from *Night of the Comet,* and while I am scared, I can take control to survive. Yeah, I'm having fun at the mall, I'm playing dress-up with my sister in the abandoned department store, but guess what? *I look just as devastating with a machine gun as I do in a ball gown.* Maybe I'm Thomasin from *The VVitch*, observing the shitty life of despair that's infected those around me and deciding to free myself of it. Who knows, maybe I'm Valerie in *Daughters of Darkness*, at first disgusted by the show of erotic power displayed by the Countess Bathory until I let loose the shackles of my relationship to a violent, masculine society and join the ranks of the eternally young, the ravishingly beautiful, and the silently powerful. Wouldn't that be nice?

Welcome to *Queer Horror*, a true labor of love that Gina and I have been working on through our zines for a few years now. Turning those zines into a full-length book is a dream come true, and I couldn't be more excited to share it with you. I hope that after you've read this book you'll come find me and tell me about it, tell me about your favorite scary movies. Write to me. I promise I'll write back!

3

THIS WAS NO BEAST

Humans and the Horror They Create

The Exorcism Department at Hallmark

JOE

You probably won't be surprised to hear this, but I've spent a lot of time thinking about *The Exorcist.* I've seen the original—many times—but I've also dipped into the entire franchise, exploring the terrible sequels, the even worse prequels, and the not-so-bad television show. It's not a big deal, and I'm not trying to impress you or anything. I watch a LOT of horror movies, and often have pretty dark storylines and ideas swirling through my head as I process them. I'm generally pretty healthy mentally: I've done my fair share of talk therapy, and I like to examine my feelings and try to deal with upsetting personal issues when they come up instead of letting them fester and rot, polluting my happiness for years to come. One thing you can't bet on, though, as a horror movie critic (or really as anyone), is when you're going to get sick. That can really throw a monkey wrench into your plans.

In 2023, I spent a month watching all of *The Exorcist* that I could find. Eventually, all that was left was the show. A TV series is a larger commitment than any one movie: it's not just a 90-120 minute movie, it's twenty 45-minute episodes—that's 900 minutes of *The Exorcist*, the equivalent of like eight movies. But these are all intricately connected, so if you space out for even just ten minutes of one episode, you might miss a lot. In order to stay with the storyline so I could write about it, I'd really been living in *The Exorcist* world . . . and then COVID hit, my second time around with this particular demon.

I don't know if you've experienced COVID (I really hope not!), but each time I've been sick with it, I've gotten *very* sick. Each illness started with a few days of intense fever, worsening so much in the evening that I'm up and down all night, in and out of a sleep so disturbed that I can't tell when I'm awake and when I'm dreaming. It's . . . not the best time to be watching a lot of *The Exorcist* media. During this particular case of COVID, I had a terrible first night of fevers, and I kept dreaming that I was working for Hallmark in their Exorcism Card Department. We were creating greeting cards that said things like "Good luck getting through your exorcism!" and "The Devil may have you now, but you're always going to be in my heart." My job, specifically, was to go observe exorcisms then come back to the card writers to discuss what it's really like, and what sentiment we needed to be sure to hit. I know, I know, it sounds ridiculous, and is quite funny in retrospect, but the experience was REALLY disturbing while it was happening. Every time I woke up, my brain on fire and seeming to push against the boundaries of my skull, I was actually worried about pleasing my bosses while dealing with the personal stress of observing real exorcisms.

That morning, I threw myself into the cozy world of the farm sim game *Stardew Valley* and decided that maybe, for the duration of the illness, at least, I'd stick to lighter media. I mean, these movies are supposed to be fiction, right?

Genderplay at the World's Fair

JOE

Have you seen *We're All Going to the World's Fair*? It's a movie steeped in the lore of creepypasta, the lore of the internet, the dark place where meme and horror meet, where the "challenges" ask you to do something more sinister than dump a bucket of ice water on your head or do a silly dance with your friends.

World's Fair is one of my favorite movies of the past few years. If you haven't seen it, I might recommend you go watch it before reading this essay. There are a lot of spoilers, and I'll be going into a deep-dive of the ending and what I think it means. If you weren't a fan of this movie, I don't mind that, and I'm not going to try to change your mind. Not every person is going to enjoy every movie that I do.

Do you know The Forecast, the early aughts Midwest emo band from Peoria, Illinois? They released one of my favorite albums from 2005, *Late Night Conversations.* In their song "These Lights," they say:

We'll drop our heads real slow to the ground
that's frozen cold and breathe it in
and move our limbs to make those wings

begin again and wait and see

what tomorrow brings.

I can't get these lyrics out of my head when I think about *We're All Going to the World's Fair*, a movie that feels so immediate and familiar to me that I think the secret to loving it is, well, being me or someone like me. I think it can be a hard movie to connect with because it *can't* resonate with everyone: for instance, I've had a much harder time touching down on director Jane Schoenbrun's next feature length, *I Saw the TV Glow (2024)*, but know a number of people this movie spoke deeply to. In a way, *World's Fair* doesn't feel like a movie to me: it's a place, it's a specific time, it's a Midwest emo song from 2005. It's a lyric you heard on your CD player while riding in the back-back of your parents' station wagon. It's a late night on the internet forums, reading scary stories that existed in a world before bots wrote half the comments. When you could trust that the comment you were replying to was, for better or for worse, written by an actual human.

In *World's Fair* we follow Casey, played phenomenally by Anna Cobb, a teenager living a lonely existence with her single father in the heart of forested, rural America; the sort of lonely woods you find in Upstate New York or deep in Michigan. She spends much of her time alone in her attic bedroom, completing viral online challenges. She becomes obsessed with one called the World's Fair Challenge, in which she must prick her finger, offer up some blood, then watch a trippy video that, according to internet legend and a number of other online videos she follows, will begin to fundamentally change her. The people online who have completed the challenge begin to change in ways that are unexpected and terrifying, becoming disconnected from their current reality, at times physically more like a fair funhouse than a human: pulling tickets from wounds on their bodies, growing clown hair. It's an unhappy challenge to take part in, and it stands in direct relation to Casey's loneliness, punctuated by director Jane Schoenbrun's decision not to introduce anyone else for most of the movie: we never see Casey's father, and she has no friends, at least none that we ever get to meet. A majority of the movie is spent watching Casey as she delicately performs the rituals of regular life: pacing around her room, skulking around the snowy exterior of her house, and talking gently, worriedly, to her imagined audience through the camera in her computer.

Over the following weeks, Casey begins to notice changes in the way she feels, but it's hard to quantify: is her recognition of a general disconnect from others a symptom of the challenge or a newfound acceptance of how she'd always felt? Did the challenge actually change her, or did it just change her perception of herself? After posting a series of increasingly disturbing videos exhibiting truly odd behavior—feeling a profound nothingness while walking in the woods, glitchy cameras recording her while she sleeps—she spends a night in her father's shed on a dusty old couch, watching comforting videos online before receiving a cryptic message from JLB, a man she learns is an advanced player in the World's Fair Challenge. He posits himself as something of an expert in the game. As they continue to correspond, and Casey descends further into madness at the hands of the World's Fair Challenge, JLB increasingly worries for her and her safety, offering to counsel her out-of-game. She, in an angry rant claiming that she "knows the World Fair is just a game" and can decide to stop participating anytime she wants, cuts off all contact with him—though not before calling him a pedophile. In an interesting directorial decision, Schoenbrun chooses to disappear Casey, and the movie ends focused entirely on JLB as narrator. In a long video follow-up, he claims to have recently met up with Casey in New York City, where she's living and thriving now (it's very difficult for me not to use Paris Hilton's portmanteau of slaying and living, *sliving*, but I resist), and though they met this once and talked like old friends, they eventually went their separate ways, content to have seen each other again and see that the other was okay. We never get to know if the meeting happened the way JLB claims, or if it even happened at all.

Which leads me to the meat of my thoughts about this movie: did *any* of this happen? We accept as a given that the movie is *about* Casey, but Casey disappears towards the end of the movie: To me, this is a movie *about* JLB. There have been a lot of theories about what happens to Casey, but I contend that Casey herself, the entirety of her life, the World's Fair Challenge, her interactions with JLB, everything we've seen in the movie, is a creepypasta *itself*.

As he's further introduced into the film, we're given incredibly intimate glimpses into JLB's life: a desk with his computer, festooned with things he likes, objects of his affection: drawings, sketches, and theories about the World's Fair Challenge, things that obviously mean a lot to him. The rest of his house, which we see him haunt around alone even though we sometimes hear his partner calling to him from another room, is meticulous and completely out of his character, as though he's caught living in another person's life but must carve out a small space in his office that's just his. We see him ignoring his partner, who calls to him from the hall, see him uncomfortably move through the perfectly untouched living room, see him alone with his phone while he uses the bathroom. He obviously inhabits this house with someone else, but he never really feels like he belongs there.

I get it. Maybe I'm classically "reading too much into" JLB's actions and life because it reminds me of how I've felt in my own life. I think the concept of feeling *invisible* never quite felt right to me. I often felt seen, just not seen as I would like to have been seen. In my book, *The Queer Affirmations Coloring Book*, I dissected my notion that common sayings, affirmations, and aphorisms actually exist to quash conversation and to end an emotional connection. JLB strikes me as someone who's also had to hear that *God helps those who help themselves* or *it's just a phase, you'll grow out of it.* What a way to misunderstand how someone is feeling!

So where *does* he belong? *We'll drop our heads real slow to the ground // that's frozen cold and breathe it in.* Does Casey even exist? Or is she just a romantic idea of how he feels, a character he relates to the most, the person he is when he's not stuck in his current life? It's no secret that director Jane Schoenbrun, who is trans, used *We're All Going to the World's Fair* as a vehicle for exploring their own coming out story. Does the World's Fair Challenge exist, or is it part of a complex creepypasta JLB created in order to explore his own gender identity? Perhaps the World's Fair represents his current existence, trapped in a life where he has to be a "man," and Casey is his attempt to reconcile how alone he feels as a differently-gendered person stuck in a life he wants to change, but doesn't know how to. Perhaps he considers Casey a form of drag, a place where he can engage in play and fantasize about how different his life could be, a character he can inhabit. But the World's Fair Challenge is changing Casey, pulling her back into her eventual life as an older man with a "normal" life, one that JLB is desperately trying to lead her away from.

Even more likely, maybe Casey is a younger version of himself who he now considers in his charge, a version of himself he's trying to calm and steward, a version who is maybe living more vibrantly than he lives now because his older self could impart some wisdom, could help set them on the, *ahem*, queer and expansive instead of the straight and narrow. Casey could only be happy by rejecting JLB and leaving the World's Fair, and maybe JLB wonders, wishes, and fanfics his own life, imagining the full and vital life he (or *she*, I should say) could have had as a younger self in the city had he learned to leave the World's Fair of his own life when he was young. Maybe Schoenbrun was engaging in a little creative genderplay of their own, living vicariously through JLB, living vicariously through Casey.

So I'm not defending this movie as one that everyone has to like or even understand. But like most queer art, there's a pain and a sensitivity that maybe people who haven't had to deal with certain things can't see. To connect to this movie feels almost blatant to me: how could I *not* see myself in it? I came out as queer when I was thirty-five. I don't consider myself a fiction writer, I don't consider myself a creepypasta aficionado, nor was I engaged in that phenomenon when it peaked over a decade ago. But this story feels so familiar to me as I explore my own feelings about gender and personal expression. This might sound silly, but the dynamic between JLB and Casey, and my theory of Casey-as-genderplay, reminds me of the deep lockdown era of the pandemic, when I'd spend hours inhabiting my island in the Nintendo video game *Animal Crossing: New Horizons.* In *ACNH,* you take part in an experiment of sorts, moving to a new resort island that's quite rough around the edges, but your existence there, and your participation in stewarding the town through many changes, leads to an island full of villagers, vibrant life, and daily ritual. My little avatar, who looked quite like me, was a great place to spend time wearing dresses, putting flowers in my hair, and letting myself feel free in a world where everyone was nice to me, all the time. It was a wonderful bit of escapism and was therapeutic at a time when I needed it. I like to think that maybe Schoenbrun, JLB, and I all feel a little better having a creative place to play.

Summer of Dread

GINA

In the summer of 1983, I was eleven years old. I loved riding my bike, reading Nancy Drew, and watching *Laverne and Shirley* and *The Jeffersons.* I'd say I was an overall happy but slightly anxious kid. I had spent the first ten years of my childhood sleeping in a bedroom not three miles away from Stateville Prison in my hometown of Joliet, Illinois. Don't get me wrong; I wasn't scared of being so close to it, nor was anyone else I knew. But you don't live that close to a federal penitentiary and not hear stories of the inmates, and for my generation of kids, those stories included Leopold and Loeb, Richard Speck, and John Wayne Gacy. I knew what these men had done; I knew alllllll the details. That's just part of what it's like to grow up in the shadow of a prison. And while, as I remember it, I was pretty able to take living down the road from Stateville in stride, some current events piled up and made it a lot harder to be a carefree kid. In 1981, Adam Walsh was kidnapped and murdered, and that well-publicized case instituted a whole new level of Stranger Danger. In the fall of 1982, the Tylenol murders happened; several folks in the Chicago area died after taking Tylenol that someone had removed from store shelves, laced with cyanide, and then put back for unsuspecting customers to buy. Because I lived in the south suburbs, that was pretty close to home for me. Then 1983 brought a threat even closer to home.

But before I get to that: Home changed for me by 1983. My family had moved from the neighborhood near Stateville to a brand-new house on the other side of the Des Plaines River in a not-yet-even-a-town-place called Homer Township, not three miles, this time, from Will-Cook Road, the road that marks the boundary line for where Will County (the county we lived in, and where our old house was) ends and Cook County (the county of which the city of Chicago is a part) begins. We had a huge yard and bigger bedrooms and were in a subdivision with gently curving streets; the only problem was, we were literally one of two houses in sight. The subdivision was only starting to develop. It was, for all intents and purposes, rural living. Our address even had a Rural Route number.

The thing about rural living that unsettled me right away is that there's a pronounced lack of people to help if you get in a jam. My partner Ellen has the exact opposite reaction to the-middle-of-nowhere places; she sees them as safe because there's a pronounced lack of bad guys: you're safe because you're alone. Yeah, I say: alone *possibly with a bad guy.* Back in 1983, I was a latch-key kid, and I worried about what would happen if I got off the school bus (I was the only one at my stop) and someone started bothering me. I missed the lights of neighboring houses at night and felt the weight of the darkness press at the windows. I won't claim I was a city kid—I didn't grow up in Chicago, after all—but town, *yes.* I was a town kid. Ok, so home wasn't in any real way more *unsafe* for me by 1983, but this anxious kid was a little more anxious.

And then something terrible happened. Well, several terrible things in a row. Near the end of June, two older women, sisters, were found shot to death in the house they shared, which was about seven miles west of my new house. The house had also been set on fire. In the first days of July, a couple was found shot to death in a car on that road I was telling you about that wasn't three miles east of my new house, Will-Cook Road. My parents wondered, the newspapers asked, I worried: Did we have a serial killer here?

In mid-July five people, including two policemen, were found shot to death on a rural road about five and a half miles north of my new house. In mid-August, a little further away, about nine miles to the south, in the nearest town to my new house, four women were stabbed and savagely mutilated in a ceramics shop. My mom's best friend knew one of those women. Evidence from a nearby car wash revealed that the killer stopped there after the murders to wash the blood off himself. We had a serial killer here.

And not *here* as in nearby, say two towns over. *Right here.* Growing up by Stateville, I knew bad people existed; because of Adam Walsh and the Tylenol murders, I knew the threat of danger was not just behind bars but out there, loose and lurking, lying in wait. But now it was *more than* just loose and lurking, lying in wait: it was circling too close to home. Like, *to my actual home.* My house, in fact, seemed like the center of a compass for the killer, who left bodies in every cardinal direction: first west, then east, then north, then south. For an anxious kid with my set of experiences, this was all some serious stuff. But I wasn't the only one who was more nervous that summer; my parents, my friends' parents, people in general in our rural area, were all more or less always on alert, always looking for suspicious people or activity. We slept uneasily and were jumpier when we heard noises we didn't recognize after dark.

The killer was dubbed the Weekend Killer because all the murders happened on weekends. If you read my essay "Lost

Girls" later in this book, you'll see that I stumbled upon *The Exorcist* on TV on a summer weekend in 1983. That weekend was in late August, after the ceramics shop killings. And that the scene of *The Exorcist* I stumbled upon wasn't, like, the party scene or one of Father Karras's tortured faith scenes or even one of the medical test scenes. I tuned in at the height of the exorcism. I didn't consciously think this at the time, but having thought a lot about it since then, I think what most harrowed me about that scene was the way it altered my perception of danger and safety. The threat of danger posed by the Weekend Killer had been circling ever closer around my house, but still, at least, like all the other threats I knew about, *outside.* But *The Exorcist* introduced the possibility of another threat, one that seemed as *internal* as was possible: how could you lock a door or bar the windows against a threat that exists *inside of you? Are you not even safe in your self?*

I remember that, in the early evening of that day I had my run-in with *The Exorcist,* my mom asked my sister and me if we wanted to go out for ice cream. There was, a few miles away, a little gift shop called Dare to Be Different, and attached to it was an ice cream shop, Dare to Be Delicious. The names, which had seemed cute to me at other times, that night took on a sinister feel: *Go on, we dare you!* I remember thinking to myself, *should we even be outside of our house?* The two shops, off a state highway, were perched on a little bluff and backed up to some woods. It was dusk when we got there. I remember standing in line at the window waiting to order my turtle sundae, then looking off into the dim woods, wondering if the Weekend Killer was peering back. Then I remembered the tormented girl in the bed, full of the devil. I don't think I had before, or have had since, a moment so utterly full of dread.

They didn't catch the Weekend Killer that summer or even that year. They did finally get him in March of 1984; his name was Milton Johnson. He murdered at least ten people in the summer of 1983 and died serving a life sentence in an Illinois prison, but not Stateville. I never watch *The Exorcist* without thinking of him and that summer.

The Bisexual Thrills of Female Vampire

JOE

I sat down in January of 2021 to watch fifty horror movies, straight from a low-budget DVD collection, and found a lot to think about. One of those movies, *Oasis of the Zombies,* is just a terrible movie. It's hard to follow, dull, and offers little to no thrills (or frills) beyond some pretty okay zombie makeup. The most exciting part of the movie comes in the first four minutes, in which we watch two young women in low-cut tops and scandalously short shorts walk hand-in-hand through the desert before succumbing to a group of zombies who are clawing their way through brush and sand (a pretty rigid interpretation of the movie title, if you ask me).

The movie interested me enough to look up the director, at least. I was not prepared for what I found in Jesús "Jess" Franco's massive catalog of self-serious, smutty movies. While some of what I watched were more akin to actual pornography than plotted movies, Franco's sex—oops, I meant to say six—decade career also seems to be filled with humor, a healthy dose of DIY, and an artful bisexuality that often errs on the side of identifying with the monster.

Now, I want to be clear that the films of his that I've seen aren't *intentionally* bisexual in a meaningful way: instead, they often follow women who occasionally have sex with other women in order to titillate a male audience. We're still seeing bisexuality through a heterosexual male lens, which is a real bummer. Sometimes, though, particularly when things were made decades ago, we have to make our own meaning and find our own inspiration through them. I found one of his films so beautiful to look at that I didn't really mind its intended hetero male gaze: 1973's *Female Vampire*, which once again teaches us not to hook up with women who materialize out of misty forests wearing only leather boots, belts, and cloaks.

In *Female Vampire*, we follow the Countess Irina Karlstein, played by the absurdly beautiful Lina Romay (who later married director Jess Franco after they'd been together for over forty years—and had made over a hundred movies together!). The Countess is mute because of a family curse . . . that also kind of weirdly makes everyone in her family a vampire. Look, curses are complicated, alright? The curse impels her to sustain her own life by sucking the life force out of her victims, which in this case is done not only by draining their blood, but also by draining their . . . well, sexual fluids. There's even a great scene that plays with a Dracula trope, in which Irina has psychic sex with a woman who's miles away by invading her mind . . . and humping a bedpost.

Anyway, there's a lot more of interest in this movie than just artful smut. As we learn through narrated diary entries, Irina is tortured by her vampiric longings and destructive nature, even when she lives in the delicious irony of her emotional-pain-for-pleasure lifestyle:

> Today is the 22nd of February, and only after a few hours of my being in Madeira, I have already killed a

> man. I earnestly wish an end would come to this bloody race that I am forced to run on this Earth through the ages. Alas, I am a prisoner. . .

So, okay, I'm watching this not-that-great, smutty, lo-fi horror movie that features lots of softcore sex scenes. Who cares? Well, there's more to it than that for me. Irina—enchanting, tortured, decidedly childfree, pansexually lusty—comes to represent the tender heart behind what could be seen as the monster of queerness, the terror of open sex. Her ghastly desires lead her to find as many victims as she'd like, most often choosing those who are similar to her—young, beautiful, and unattached—finding a family of those most like herself to connect with, to share intimate experiences with. Her longing to be normal is everlasting, but she can't be normal. Blending in is just not who she is. Though Irina is ravishingly beautiful, often clad in fine clothing and never afraid to show off her feminine form, her hard stare, muteness, and odd affect make it hard for her to connect with others. She stalks around powerfully, each step taken with purpose, regardless of how casual and alluring she makes it look. She rarely lets anyone take her power, which is a hard thing to uphold for someone marginalized: You can *feel* those around her trying to figure her out, but they will never be able to. Her "curse" will only allow her to kill her victims through pure pleasure, casting her as the demon of desire. What is it about Irina that is cursed? Is she really a vampire who spreads death for her own selfish needs? Or is she just a free-spirited bi-babe who could only be *understood* as a monster?

We even see Irina fighting with her circumstances in a way that feels all-too-familiar to anyone who has fought with their own sexuality. There is one woman Irina desires, one she loves and can't bear to kill: a reporter she meets poolside at a resort in Madeira. After doing an interview together, one in which the reporter asks the mute Irina to answer questions about her supposed-vampiric heritage by nodding yes or no, Irina calls to her in the night (another classic Dracula trope), and instead of simply invading her mind, she has psychic sex with her. When the longing becomes too much she eventually flies to her room as a bat, transforms back into a human, and initiates the real thing.

After she seduces the reporter, the Countess walks back into the woods where we first met her, striding through the fog in her iconic boots-belt-cloak combo. Only this time, the reporter is following her, naked as well except for a pair of chunky-heeled white crinkle boots. For a moment, we get to believe that Irina has finally found love, found someone she can be with, without killing her. Alas, in the next scene, while Irina drives down the mountain from her ancestral home—alone, I might add, for we never see the reporter again (she seemingly comes to the same fate as all of Irina's other lost loves)—she laments her situation: why can't she have love? Why can't she be with the one she desires? She slinks back to her hotel room to masturbate, a frenzied, shameful session that speaks to her want: who *does* she love? Is she so ashamed of her desire that she needs to pleasure herself alone in her room?

Female Vampire exemplifies what can be so great about smutty seventies movies, beginning with the aesthetic. The warm, soft grain of the film, shot mostly in natural light among the verdant leafy mountains surrounding Madeira, Portugal, presents a lush and inviting landscape, a place that feels quiet and peaceful but modern at the same time. The slow scenes that sprawl across the film: the long drives up and down the mountain, the camera positioned out the front windshield, focusing on a flapping car hood ornament and the cars that drive by; the extended shots of the Countess as she slowly stands from her bed, naked except for a long, black cloak that she pulls around her and throws behind her into the air, softly trailing behind her; the languid jungles that surround the city, their giant leaves bowing listlessly in the humid air. But the movie isn't deadly serious, as lots of the dialogue is so odd as to be terribly funny, though it's hard to tell if it was intentional or not: "What a strange house, it looks like a tomb. Is it the house of your ancestors?" says the mustachioed Jack Taylor, playing a psychic investigator who is sure he is the true love of the Countess's life. The dialogue becomes ever more poetic, most likely because of the translation. Take this exchange between the forensic scientist Dr. Roberts (played by director Franco) and his colleague, Dr. Orloff, while they examine another female victim of the vampire:

> Dr. Orloff: The two canines have pierced the lips and deformed the clitoris. That's what the first vampires did, sucking the life energy and leaving their victims bloodless.
>
> Dr. Roberts: What you say is more than terrifying, the demons must be killed. And it must be . . . forever.
>
> Dr. Orloff: What for? How are we to know that the pleasure isn't worth life itself?

To think, the idea that sexual pleasure could be worth life itself. Worth fighting for, perhaps, or at the very least, worth keeping your goddamn snout out of if it doesn't make any difference to your own life.

As silly as this might sound, movies like *Female Vampire* are actually important: it's important to have movies other than straight-up pornography in which a character can enjoy sex that lies outside of mainstream heteronormative acceptability. To acknowledge that sex other than steamy, panting, hetero sex even *exists.* We're lucky today to have so many movies that proudly call themselves queer, that queer horror is a genre tag we can use to describe more than just a handful of movies. It's even more important that enjoyable, free, bisexual sex was just one piece of this movie, and not the central theme—Franco didn't set out to make a movie to champion the queer experience, but here I am, fifty years later, giving *Female Vampire* the blue ribbon for doing just that. The Countess may have been a vampire who was killing her victims, but what was she actually killing? Maybe it was a massacre of conventional norms, a slaying of patriarchal hetero ideals. To that I say: slay, Irina, slaaaaaay.

While *Female Vampire* was likely made with straight men in mind, I can't help but feel that, as a larger group, the straight-and-narrows are most likely uninterested in keeping this arty seventies softcore horror film for themselves, and I feel confident saying that *Female Vampire* now belongs to us. With a jaunty seventies score, aesthetically interesting cinematography, and enough arresting visuals of Lina Romay to stop your heart, *Female Vampire* is a surprisingly fun watch—if you're feeling daring enough to get a little saucy.

PS: I want to tell you in case you're looking to watch this on your own, the director decided to release the film in three different versions: *Female Vampire* is the version I'm describing, a balanced version which blends horror and sex, which Franco released to appeal to more casual fans. *The Bare-Breasted Countess* is the original version, one that's light on horror and heavy on sex. Franco was originally interested in only producing dirty movies. And finally, *Erotikill* features the horror elements but not much sex, which Franco believed would give the movie more mass appeal, but which turned out to be a major dud. I recommend watching *Female Vampire.* I mean, if you're just looking to watch a nudie movie, you can do MUCH better than *The Bare-Breasted Countess,* and the movie is hardly scary enough to warrant just being a horror movie, which rules *Erotikill* out.

Regan MacNeil and Other Possessed Girls Strapped to Beds

GINA

Among all the ways that the 1973 classic movie *The Exorcist* changed the horror genre—and there are so many—one that's definitely underappreciated is that it spawned a legion of possessed girls strapped to beds.

Regan MacNeil, full of the devil and tied to her bed, is a spectacle. Even when she's at her ugliest—*especially* when she's at her ugliest—we can't look away. Her nightgown is caked with vomit, her face mottled with bruises and cuts, her lips dry and cracked. She spews profanities, moans like she's dying, and talks backwards. She demands sexual acts from the priests trying to help her, even from her mother. She's just *a lot.* Film scholar Kendall R. Phillips has made a claim about one of the ways that horror works on us that explains why Regan packs such a punch: "The violation of an audience's expectations," he says, "contributes to their experience of terror and, in so doing, redraws the contours of the horror genre."

Yes. Regan represented an entirely new way of using children in general, but especially young girls in horror movies. Before her there were tidy, extremely capable blond kids like Rhoda in

The Bad Seed and the alien kids in *Village of the Damned*, but these children were creepy rather than horrifying. They weren't hard to look at or listen to. Regan *really is*, and a large part of what makes her so troubling is that she doesn't look and act like we expect a young girl to look and act.

And make no mistake, Regan works as well as she does as a character because she's a girl. Here's a fact you might not know: *The Exorcist* is actually based on a real-life exorcism that William Peter Blatty, author of the novel and also the screenplay, studied when he was in college. That exorcism was performed in 1949 on a young *boy* from Maryland. Why did Blatty change the sex of the possessed child for his story? One reason I've read about is that he was told in no uncertain terms by the Catholic church *not* to write a story about that 1949 exorcism, and, well, if he wasn't writing about a possessed *boy*, that was an indication that he was following orders.

But I think a much more convincing reason why Blatty made this change is that a young girl offered a more titillating subject. The truth is, there just aren't a lot of gripping stories about male characters facing the devil in our culture: Christoper Marlowe's *Doctor Faustus*, Washington Irving's *The Devil and Tom Walker*, Stephen Vincent Benet's *The Devil and Daniel Webster*? They're all interesting enough, but as horror? Nope. Even films like *Devil's Advocate* and *Event Horizon*, to say nothing of that masterpiece of a song, "The Devil Went down to Georgia" by the Charlie Daniels Band: These are all more examples of dramas than horror, and certainly not innovative horror. To return to Phillips' idea, they don't violate our expectations. And here's something interesting: in all of them, the male characters facing the devil do so not strapped to beds in a forced passive position but in active and often purely intellectual ways, usually making deals or having arguments with him. Rarely are female characters in stories with the devil given such opportunities; indeed, rarely are they allowed the dignity of even meeting the devil standing up. If you ask me, Blatty saw there was just something far more vulnerable about a young possessed girl. He sensed that, if the devil were inside *her*, she would get inside audiences in ways a possessed boy just couldn't.

He was right. There's something about a girl strapped to a bed and threatened by the devil that we as a culture just *cannot* get enough of; she evokes fears related to gendered violence, violence against self, loss of self-control, impurity, illness, powerlessness—the list goes on and on. And we can't stop perseverating on these fears; we return to them again and again. Movies about demonic possession are movies about girls strapped to beds: *The Exorcism of Emily Rose; Exorcism: The Possession of Gail Bowers; The Last Exorcism; The Devil Inside; The Possession; The Possession of Hannah Grace;* and I'm positive that's just a partial list. All these movies, all the female characters whose stories they tell, carry the legacy of Regan MacNeil. Her character didn't just *help* define, it *singlehandedly* defined the trope of the possessed girl in horror. The frequency of this trope alone, the way it has come to dominate horror stories about the devil, demonstrates the power of that depiction of poor Regan strapped to her bed.

But it wasn't just in the long run that the potency of that character's plight became apparent. It happened right away, in the movie *The Exorcist* itself. Regan stole the show from those priests trying to help her. Look at that list of movies above and notice that their focus is on the possessed girl, the possession itself, or the exorcism. Those are the subjects named in the titles, the nouns used. Now think back to the movie that inspired them all: *The Exorcist.* Not *The Possessed Girl,* not *The Exorcism of Regan MacNeil.* The movie's title points to the priests! Father

Merrin and Father Karras are meant to be the main protagonists of *The Exorcist.* The movie does a lot to center them as the devil's main opponents. It's clear that an ancient enmity exists between the devil and Father Merrin; the opening scenes suggest he's circling the elderly priest, waiting for his moment to strike. Later in the movie, when Father Merrin enters the MacNeil house, the devil bellows his name from upstairs, suggesting he's been waiting eagerly, even hungrily, for his old opponent to arrive. For his part, Father Karras is in the grips of a crisis of faith from the start to the end of the movie, so much so that he truly might never even really wholeheartedly believe that Regan is actually possessed, even when the devil uses her to torment him about his struggles with belief and his guilt over the recent death of his mother. Father Karras's faith is wavering; the devil wants to stamp it out completely. He has set his sights on these priests; he wants to take them down. Regan is tangled up in their struggles with him, and she's surely meant to demonstrate the devil's depravity, but she was only meant to be a vessel for the devil to fill, to use, maybe to break. And it might be that's all Regan ever was in the movie. But even as a vessel, she upstages the priests in active battle with the devil. When you think of *The Exorcist,* whose face do you immediately see? Most people who aren't superfans probably couldn't even confidently pick the priests out of a lineup, but even people who haven't seen the movie know who Regan is.

Regan also wrestled the story away from its creators. Famously, Blatty refused to acknowledge that *The Exorcist* is a horror story; he understood it to be a drama about faith, and the movie's director, William Friedkin, stood with him on this point. Both of them saw the priests' stories as primary and, by doing so, maybe without even realizing it, underestimated Regan's character. Sure, they expected that audiences would be tantalized by her, but they didn't seem to realize that she would become more than just a *part* of the story; that she had it in her to be *the main story*. Not to mention that, by being the main story, she would help define a genre—a genre they weren't even looking to contribute to—for decades to come.

Turns out a girl strapped to a bed has a lot of power.

PS: In 2023, I made a podcast about *The Exorcist*. It's called *Taking on the Devil: Celebrating 50 Years of The Exorcist*. It's available on most streaming platforms. Give it a listen if you want to hear more about Regan and the priests who try to help her.

The Delight of Spotting Himbos in the Wild

JOE

I'm not well-versed in the long and presumably illustrious history of the horror himbo—you know, the handsome, studly fella who's all brawn and no brain, all looks and no books, all sexy and no savvy—but I've been tickled by the term ever since I first heard it, reveling in the dopey boyfriends of 2009's *Sorority Row* and the mid-eighties fascination with beautiful men who just can't keep up. [See Johnny Depp's Glen, the sweetly dopey, slack-and-sweater-vest-wearing, bouffanted boyfriend in *Nightmare on Elm Street* (1984) and Caleb, the rugged boy who misses all the right clues from *Near Dark* (1987).] Wikipedia tells me that himbo is a newer term, coined most likely in the 1980s. It seems the term bimbo was once gender neutral but began to take on feminine connotations in the twentieth century, and thus, the word himbo was born as a counterbalance.

So what a charming surprise it is to stumble upon himbos in the wild, like Rob Estes's Peter in 1989's *Phantom of the Mall: Eric's Revenge* and basically all of the men in 1984's *The Cold (aka The Game). Phantom of the Mall: Eric's Revenge* is an incredibly silly retelling of *The Phantom of the Opera.* (Also of importance: the movie features a really charming young Pauly Shore). Technically, Peter is a pretty important character, unraveling the evil plan that runs through the heart of the plot so one could surmise this means he's not a *true* himbo, but I like to think this unique twist only serves to add depth to the himbo as an archetype—one who, sometimes unwittingly, is capable of great things.

The Cold, a pretty benign straight-to-VHS film in which a group of millionaires torment and haunt contestants in a game of their own making, is a little less kind to the handsome gentlemen found within. What fun it was to find myself in the pleasing company of silly, studly men—with their mustaches and muscles, their late-seventies-even-though-it's-the-eighties haircuts, their too-tight jeans—generally loping around and goofing off while the women took charge. *The Cold* won't wow you with its stilted acting, goofy frights, and hazy air of late-seventies softcore pornography (it's just a vibe, though—there isn't any sex, though there is some nudity), but I found the movie entertaining enough to lazily watch on a hot summer's afternoon.

It's easy to find listicles around the internet telling you about the "Ten Handsomest Himbos in Horror," but it's much harder to find good examples of their appearances prior to the 1980s, so I went digging. And boy did I find some simple and stunning men! Horror has a long history of bringing hunky, fanciable simpletons to the screen for us all to take in and admire. From the handsome, careless actions of Penderel in 1932's *Old Dark House* to the dopey choices made by the dadly-good-looking Watson Pritchard in 1959's *House on Haunted Hill*, it seems there are examples of silly male eye candy characters going back to the very invention of film.

Perhaps one of the greatest (and most interesting) himbos in horror was Gomez Addams, as portrayed by John Astin in

The Addams Family television show from the 1960s. (Cute sidenote: in his forward to the 1991 book *The Addams Chronicles*, Astin admits to "razoring selected cartoons for framing" from Addams' cartoons when he was in college). Gomez is fanciable and debonair, devoted to his dear Morticia, and—though he's worth a great deal of money—he also makes absolutely terrible business and personal decisions, depending on a phenomenal amount of luck and whimsy to guide him instead of any kind of acumen or knowledge.

In the fifth episode of the series, "The Addams Family Tree," a neighboring oil magnate, Mr. Pomeroy, believes a piece of land Gomez owns is rich with oil. As he negotiates to purchase the land, the Addamses extol the man's unsavory family tree (they love his family's history of bad deeds, naturally!), a bit of information they gleaned while having their own family history done by a local historian. Pomeroy believes Gomez is extorting him, which leads him to offer well more than the property could ever be worth. (Spoiler alert: Gomez later acknowledges there's not a drop of oil in the land while praising Pomeroy for being so kind, thinking he purchased the land to apologize for once calling the Addamses kooks). It might be hard to think of a sweet-talking billionaire as a himbo, but if you watch the show through a himbo-lens (a Himblense™), you'll see him for what he is: a bumbling weirdo who we all just love to look at.

On my latest watching of *The Addams Family*, I really focused on Gomez as a character and his relationships when an unexpected question arose: Is Gomez a familiar of Morticia's? Morticia herself is a wonderful character. With a name derived from the word mortician, she's a terrifyingly confident witchy vampiress who, in a 1991 interview from *The Addams Chronicles*, Charles Addams admits is modeled after actress Gloria Swanson, perhaps best known today for her role of Norma Desmond in the fantastically off-kilter *Sunset Boulevard.* Morticia spends a good portion of the series swanning around their mansion elegantly, bemused by her husband's constant doting and seeing him through the financial ups-and-downs of his businesses. (Not that it matters; Gomez is thought to have more money than anyone would ever need. In 2007, Forbes published a humorous article in which they valued all of his properties and businesses at a total net worth of $2.5 billion, adjusted for today's inflation.) It isn't until 1991's *The Addams Family* movie that we learn that Gomez and Morticia met at a funeral, so entranced with each other that hardly anyone could pay attention to the funeral at hand, instead focusing on Gomez as he sunk so deeply in love that he proposed to Morticia on that spot. Is he simply a lovesick loon, or was he enchanted by Morticia through supernatural means? Perhaps most damning of all the evidence is that, according to the 1964 sitcom, Gomez was known to be a sickly boy, often taken to bed in poor health, only finding his great vitality once he'd met Morticia. Is this the vim and vigor of true love's kiss or a transfer of vampiric power? We've yet to find out, but the more I learn about their relationship and his utter devotion, the more it seems that magic may well be involved.

Regardless of the specifics of their relationship, Gomez Addams—particularly as played by John Astin—stands as a shining example of the perfect himbo: handsome and athletic, always up for adventure but with a childlike sense of wonder and whimsy, and so damn rich that he never needs to give a thought to spending whatever amount of money he desires.

So here's to horror's unsung hero, the himbo, who so often adds humor and a touch of charm when we need a break from being haunted. Whether he's getting the ax—quite literally—or playing a love-struck fool, I always look forward to a himbo gracing my screen (and, eventually, taking off his shirt).

Who Is She? Quick Horror Recs on the Theme of Human Monsters from Joe

Lizzie (Craig William Macneill, 2018)

The murder of Lizzie Borden's parents was so gruesome and mysterious that humanity as a whole is tortured by still not actually knowing what happened. We know a few things: during the morning of August 4, 1892, Lizzie Borden's stepmother Abby was slaughtered with an ax in her second floor bedroom, and roughly an hour later, Lizzie's father Andrew, who had only recently come home and didn't know his wife was upstairs, dead, was murdered with an ax as well, while napping on the living room couch. There are so many theories about what could have happened. Lizzie explores one of those theories, and one of the best ones: in this telling, Lizzie (Chloë Sevigny) and the family maid Bridget (Kristen Stewart) worked together to murder Lizzie's terrible parents because they were in love and wanted not only freedom from their oppression but also to inherit Andrew Borden's great wealth. *Lizzie* is a pretty solid movie and features some steamy scenes, in addition to a legitimately tense atmosphere—but trigger warning, there are some heavy allusions to sexual assault. I liked the acting a lot, and the quietude of the movie really spoke to how awfully difficult life could be back then. Chloë Sevigny and Kristen Stewart are two of my faves, and they both seem hilariously anachronistic to that time, which is kind of a hoot to watch. Like, I'm sorry, but you two are just totally out of place in the 1800s, lol!

Daughters of Darkness (Harry Kümel, 1971)

I bought this movie at a thrift store on DVD, packaged without its box in a simple white paper sleeve. I hadn't ever heard of it but figured it must be pretty good with a name like that. It was only a buck; I mean, why not give it a shot? Katie and I watched it one night, and then watched it again just a few nights later. I wanted to live inside of this movie. A newlywed couple, Stefan and Valerie, travel by train on their honeymoon to an opulent hotel on the Belgian coast. While there, they have some . . . disturbing sex, then meet the entrancing Countess Elizabeth Báthory and her secretary, Ilana. The Countess soon has her eyes on Valerie and has to remove Stefan from the picture to have her. *Daughters of Darkness* is a gothic masterpiece. It's quiet, it's sexy, it's entrancing. It's also really gay in the most splendid ways: oh, just wait until you meet Stefan's mother! I've since bought the special edition DVD, and even picked up the soundtrack on vinyl, which we play out our front window every Halloween.

Sunset Boulevard (Billy Wilder, 1950)

If you don't feel scared while watching this movie, then I don't know what to tell you. It's the kind of scared you get watching *Mommie Dearest* or *Grey Gardens. Sunset Boulevard* is a dark comedy from 1950 that follows an aging actress, Norma Desmond (played by Gloria Swanson) whose sun has set on her career. She manipulates a down-on-his-luck scriptwriter to keep him close, trapping him in a romantic relationship that he may never escape, all the while attempting to resurrect her career while spooking around her dilapidated mansion. *Sunset Boulevard* is a gorgeous movie, the set lush and full, the drama heightened and tense. It's a fantastic film that's been given countless accolades since its release. You should watch it!

Butcher, Baker, Nightmare Maker (later released as *Night Warning*) (William Asher, 1982)

This movie was not going to get a recommendation from me until I saw the final scene. It's so, so gratifying. Here's the movie in a nutshell: a teenager's parents die an untimely death so he goes to live with his aunt, who has an unhealthy obsession with him. His life degenerates because of her fixation, and a lot of slasher-esque shit goes down. It's pretty entertaining all the way through, but it isn't a comedy, and let me tell you, this one has NOT aged well. Not that some of the homophobic slurs and ideas should have even been acceptable then, either. It's actually kind of a good story, which I feel a bit ridiculous to admit. There's lots of drama, good guys and bad guys, some gory kills, some overacting, and some really zany scenes. You'll have to suffer through some intense anti-queer sentiments and slurs to get to it, but there is some sweet, sweet revenge awaiting the bad guys to make it (almost?) worthwhile.

Sisters of Death (Joe Mazzuca, 1977)

While *Sisters of Death* isn't a very exciting movie, I love the mood and the drama of it: the drifting, listless shots of seventies girls' thighs; the lurid gaze of the overdramatic men; the convoluted storyline. The story follows a secret society of women, sort of like a coven, The Sisters (of Death), who, during an initiation of two members, accidentally use a pistol loaded with real bullets instead of blanks, killing one of the initiates. They find themselves in need of a vacation, and sun themselves in some sort of desert pool paradise resort while being watched and then hunted by the deranged father of the slain initiate; they can't escape because, naturally, they're trapped by a high-voltage electric fence. (What kind of resort is this??) This could be a stage play adapted from a Grecian odyssey, hazily bathed in the sexiness of the seventies, hot on the heels of movies like *Daughters of Darkness* and *The Velvet Vampire.* I should make a point to say there's no actual sex in *Sisters of Death,* but there are some artful shots of naked women, some women clothed in flouncy tops and short, short skirts, and lots of hair. The warmth of the old film adds to the feeling of smuttiness, even though it only nods winkingly to actual smut, with the entire movie bathed in a lo-fi, dirty atmosphere.

Salvation! (Rose Glass, A24, 2021)

Salvation! is a zine by Rose Glass, creator and director of the films *Saint Maud* and *Love Lies Bleeding* from A24—who not only produced this film but also released the zine. The zine serves as a vision board and companion piece to *Saint Maud,* featuring disturbing original art, short form essays by Glass, reproductions of intense art pieces offered up for reflection, and stark religious photography juxtaposed against vintage smut, antique newspaper ads, and thoughtfully poetic reveries. *Salvation!* offers a deeper cultural context for *Saint Maud,* but is an arresting piece of art when it stands alone, too.

Ghosts I Have Seen and Other Psychic Experiences (Violet Tweedale, New York: F.A. Stokes Co., 1919)

This book is a really interesting look into the everyday experiences of a Victorian spiritualist. Violet Tweedale is awesome: She was an early Scottish feminist, spiritualist who dabbled in early forms of Satanism. She was a vocal supporter of women's rights, a critic of high society, and an early ghost hunter, spending time leading seánces in haunted spaces or simply walking the halls of a dark, spooky mansion with her father or husband. In *Ghosts I Have Seen*, Tweedale recounts the spirits that surround her and pervade high society functions—from the mediums who speak to them to the demons who attach themselves to (literally) haunted war veterans and the spirits of socialites past who still walk through grand gardens and castle halls. With her ultra-progressive views and one foot always firmly planted in the spiritual world, I can't help but feel that, if Tweedale were alive today, she'd be acting as *Grand Dame* of the queer ghost hunting world. Much is made of queer speculation through the ages, and Tweedale is a fun person to speculate about: she was independent, sporty (an avid and celebrated golfer in her time), strong-willed, physically imposing, and seemingly not afraid to make her voice heard in male spaces—not to mention she had a number of female friends that she spent days, sometimes weeks, in the company of. *Ghosts I Have Seen* can be a little dry to read straight through mostly because of its age, but the essays stand on their own, and it's an interesting artifact of a specific time and interest.

The Blackcoat's Daughter (Oz Perkins, 2015)

Some movies are all about atmosphere. In *The Blackcoat's Daughter*, two girls are left mostly alone at a prep school over a week-long break. The only adults present are two nurses. One girl meets Satan, gets along well with him, goes on a killing spree. Also sort of goes on a killing spree in the future? I don't know, the timeline gets sloppy and at times it was hard for me to follow. The movie starts out as kind of a slow burn, with lots of talking and long shots of desolate scenery and meaningful looks. It picks up, but yeesh, there's lots of loud, bleating synth noises and one-way dialogue—why doesn't anyone answer anyone in this movie? The grotesqueness of the movie goes a little far—the kill scenes are just brutal, and sometimes not in a fun way. But in spite of all its flaws, the movie has excellent momentum: Kiernan Shipka is awesomely creepy as Kat, and I love the representation of the devil. I also love the mounting and constant tension between Kat and Emma Roberts's Joan. Too many movies are about devil worshippers and cultists, in which you ultimately meet a goat-headed demon, but rarely do they make a truly scary, understated, and eerie devil like this one. He is but a shadow, a lingering thought whispered from the furnace. The production's good, the movie's beautiful, and the pacing is nice, when it isn't interrupted by those pesky future events. Maybe this is just me being persnickety, but I also didn't love the idea that the movie felt more akin to the experience of living in the seventies than the aughts, when it actually took place. Why were the school nurse uniforms so old-timey? And the decor of every building, except the dorm, was totally unchanged in thirty-five years? Weird, man. Maybe I just don't know anything about prep schools—spoiler alert, I don't. Or maybe it was just an artistic choice to confuse the viewer, blurring the lines between past and present. Anyway, worth a watch if you're feeling quiet and eerie, but get ready for a few really brutal attack scenes!

The Midnight Swim (Sarah Adina Smith, 2014)

So, I like this movie very much. It had a pace I enjoyed; I liked the actors, the quiet atmosphere, and the mystery. The characters feel like real sisters, an accomplishment all its own, and the film does a good job examining trust, guilt, and personal reflection. It gave me a lot to chew on: I'm a big reader of mythology, and I was happy to jump back in and re-read the story of the Pleiades after watching this. You could spend a lot of time with this movie. Small synopsis: three sisters meet at their mother's house to deal with the will and all that after their mother's death. The sisters have a hard time breaking their old patterns of communication, and the youngest seems to be losing herself bit by bit to a mystery that she believes surrounds her mother's death in the local lake. It's a real slow burn, so you have to be in the mood for a quiet film centered mostly around talking. Unsettling is the word that best describes it. It's not queer per se: it's not a story about queer love, or even about queer people. But some of the lessons learned, the story told, really spoke to me at a time when I was digging into my feelings and exploring my own gender identity and burgeoning queerness.

And a Few Quick Recs from Gina, Too

Saint Maud (Rose Glass, 2019)

Hospice nurse and zealous Catholic Maud provides end-of-life care for cancer patient Amanda, who's not religious. Maud tends to Amanda's needs not just with physical care but by trying to save her soul. Complicating this for Maud is Carol, the sex worker who visits Amanda. Maud bans Carol from the house so Amanda can focus on spiritual matters, and that goes as well as you'd expect. Things escalate; Amanda calls Maud a homophobe. She's not wrong, but she's particularly nasty about it, and her nastiness doesn't stop there. Her meanness makes it hard to be on her side, which is uncomfortable because you *definitely* don't want to be on Maud's side. So who's the hero, and who's the villain? In their own heads, both Maud and Amanda are the hero opposing the other's villain, but buying either one's version of the conflict is complicated by many factors. Ultimately, one of them does seem to prevail. But then, *literally* the last second of the film snatches it away from her. It's worth a watch for that last second alone, but be warned: that last second isn't for the faint of heart.

What Keeps You Alive (Colin Minihan, 2018)

Married couple Jules and Jackie celebrate their one-year anniversary at Jackie's family cabin. It's isolated, but not so isolated: a neighbor from across the lake sees lights on and comes to check why. That neighbor is Jackie's childhood friend Sarah, who calls Jackie by a different name, Megan. Suspicious, Jules asks Jackie about it; she explains she changed her name when she came out. But Jules' suspicions grow when she rows across the lake alone to visit Sarah and learns about another friend, Jenny, who drowned in the lake swimming with Jackie/Megan. Sarah is visibly stunned that Jackie/Megan never mentioned Jenny to Jules—and so is Jules. These early revelations are just the tip of the iceberg: Jackie/Megan turns out to be real trouble. At one point, Jules asks her, "What turned you into this monster?" Jackie/Megan replies: "It's nature, not nurture." So, the message is that Jackie/Megan was *born this way?* Kinda a problematic way to characterize a lesbian character, even if she is the villain. Jules, though, is the goods. At first you wonder why she's paired up with a sociopath, but once *she* realizes she is, she becomes a formidable force.

Alone with You (Emily Bennett & Justin Brooks, 2021)

Charlie waits for her girlfriend Simone to return from out of town in the apartment they share and where the movie unfolds. The place has several escalating issues that make it creepy: a shadowy figure unseen by Charlie and barely seen by us; abject sobbing from the apartment next door which Charlie (and we) hear through the vents; and a door—the only door—that refuses to open, trapping Charlie inside. More unsettling vibes come from the drunk friend who keeps calling Charlie saying how awful Simone is; a surprise video call to Charlie from her churchy mom; and Charlie leaving message after message for Simone, who never answers and never comes home. Simone seems dubious at best and sinister at worst, but we never get our own look at her, so drawing conclusions is hard. Charlie doesn't look great either; she vacillates between seeming pathetic and deluded, but always, more or less volatile and dangerous—though since she's alone in the apartment, only to herself? This is definitely Charlie's story, but is she the hero or the villain? It's hard to say because *nothing really happens* in this movie.

THIS IS A HOUSE OF HORRORS

Horror About Scary Places and Haunted Houses

How to Draw a Haunted House

GINA

It was a fall afternoon in 1981 in Joliet, Illinois. I sat at the kitchen table with my crayons and markers and the blank 12 x 18-inch piece of paper every fourth grader had been given that day at school in front of me. My class was having a Halloween art contest, and I was talking to my mom about it, trying to decide what to draw.

"Draw a haunted house," she said. "My dad taught me how to draw one, and I'll show you."

My mom's dad—my grandpa Andy—had died suddenly two years before. He had owned and tended a neighborhood tavern with my grandma Sophie until he died. He was handsome, and he liked to fish. That's mostly what I knew about him, except that he definitely didn't seem like the kind of guy who would know how to draw—or even care about drawing—a haunted house. I was shocked and impressed. Flitting between the kitchen counter where she was preparing dinner and the table where I was hunched over my big piece of paper, my mom talked me through the steps the way he had done with her when she was a kid.

"First draw a big hill, but leave room for the house at the top." My green marker started low on the left side of the paper and sloped steeply up on its way to the right side.

"Now put some gravestones on the hillside," and I did, even putting some names and birth and death dates on them. I threw in a cross for good measure.

"Add a rickety fence, a pumpkin vine, a creepy tree, and the moon." Done, done, done, and done.

"Now draw the house." I based my house on the Weebles Haunted House toy my little sister Amy and I had—do you remember Weebles, the little, bottom-heavy figurines that wobbled but never fell down? I *loved* that toy haunted house, which, I realized when I grew up and saw the movie, had to be an homage to Norman Bates's house in *Psycho.* Like the Weebles haunted house, mine had a mansard roof and a boarded-up front window. I added a pumpkin by the front door and some cobwebs in the eaves.

According to my mom, who, despite the passage of over forty years since she helped me with this drawing, remembered these directions with startling clarity, the characters in the drawing were all my idea: I added a ghost over the house letting out a big BOO!, a witch flying toward the moon, a bat, a yellow-eyed owl in the tree and a black cat perched on the fence.

I took care with my drawing—you can see the pencil lines I made to rough in some parts of it. I used marker, pencil, and crayon. I paid attention to small details: my house has intricate scalloped shingles on the roof, my witch has a wart on her nose and green hair, and my tree has a dark hollow in its trunk.

The drawing is on my desk as I write this. I've kept it all these years, carrying it with me from one city to the next, one apartment to the next, finally to a house of my own (no mansard roof, no boarded-up window). My drawing won the contest, but that's not why I keep it—maybe that's why I did at first, but now I have a different reason. It's the product of these now generations-old directions, which are a kind of inheritance passed from my grandpa, through my mom, to me: like a cherished family recipe, a secret potion, or a magic spell. A spooky legacy.

GINA BRANDOLINO, GRADE 4

Lesbian Ghost

GINA

As a kid, I was captivated by the movie *Poltergeist.* It came out in 1982, when I was 10; I didn't see it until it went to video, but then I made my parents rent the VHS tape for me *over and over.* It's still one of my all-time favorite movies. It tells the story of the Freelings, a young, happy family of five who are living the suburban dream until things get weird in their house: glasses break, forks bend, furniture moves—all of their own accord. A giant tree grabs one of the kids through a window, then another kid—the youngest, Carol Anne—just . . . disappears. Seems to evanesce into the house. The Freelings can hear her voice through the television, but no matter how hard or how frantically they look for her, she's nowhere to be found. It's hard to find people to help with problems like these; unfortunately, the Freelings were two years too early and, even then, in the wrong movie for "Who ya gonna call?" "Ghostbusters!" They do eventually find an awesome parapsychologist, Dr. Lesh, who tries to help and quickly admits she's out of her league. Then Dr. Lesh brings in the even more awesome spiritual medium Tangina Barrons, who is *not* out of her league. Yep, she confirms: ya got ghosts, and also something else much, much nastier than a ghost along with them, and they've got Carol Anne.

I don't know if any of the ghosts in the Freelings' house are lesbians. Probably some of them were; there were *a lot* of them, after all. This essay isn't so much about those ghosts as, well, *me*. I'm the lesbian ghost of the title. I grew up in the 1970s and 1980s in a working-class family in a working-class town. I didn't have any models for adulthood that weren't straight; I didn't know I wasn't straight myself, really, until I was twenty-four years old, when I came out. I always knew I wasn't going to have a life like the lives of the women I knew—having a husband and kids wasn't even a thing I could envision. Increasingly in my early twenties, this made me feel *off*, *wrong* in inexplicable and certainly inarticulable ways. It's hard to find people to help with problems like these.

Tangina explains to the Freelings that the ghosts rattling around their house are trapped between this life and the next. "These souls who for whatever reason are not at rest are also not aware that they have passed on," she says. "They're not part of consciousness as we know it. They live in a perpetual dream state, a nightmare from which they cannot awaken." It's a surprisingly spot-on description of what it feels like, not so much to be in the closet, but *to not even realize* you're in the closet, but to know something's . . . *not right*. You don't really connect with the people around you; you don't share a lot of their hopes and goals, or even their tastes and tendencies. You are kind of a ghost, caught in a terrible, lonely limbo.

Spoiler alert: I'm about to give away a lot about how *Poltergeist* winds up. Tangina knows how to help the ghosts in the Freelings' house. What it comes down to is, the ghosts got lost on the way to the light—the "spectral light," Tangina calls it. They need to find it again and pass into it, she explains, "where friends are waiting to guide them to new destinies." Tangina doesn't *think* she knows what's going on; she *knows*, and best of all, she explains it with bracing frankness and clarity. She's one of the most charismatic, centered, potent characters in any movie, horror or otherwise. She's a fantastic medium; she *gets* what's going on in the Freelings' house; she *understands* the ghosts, *acknowledges* them, *empathizes* with them. She *helps* them. You know what she is? She's an ally. And *wow*, are allies valuable.

I had two allies that helped me when I needed it most, two straight people who couldn't ever say they'd been in my shoes before but seemed to know exactly what to do to help me. One was my friend Kate, whom I met the year before I came out and who held my hand through that transition. When my first girlfriend dumped me, Kate went to the lesbian bar with me. She listened to me cry and rage without impatience or judgment. She made up a nickname for my ex so mean I won't even share it here, but needless to say, that buoyed me up. And she made me laugh and gave me confidence.

My other ally was my little sister Amy, who managed the unmitigated disaster that my coming out to our parents turned out to be. (Because it doesn't always happen, it's worth mentioning that my parents have both, in the years since I came out, also become allies in their own ways.) It's hard to do justice to the iron fist Amy wielded in those days, but here's one example: I came out specifically because Amy wanted my girlfriend to be able to come with me to her wedding. This went over especially badly with my mom, who whipped herself up into a frenzy thinking about how my sister's wedding was her only chance to be the mother of the bride. She only had two kids! One ended up being a lesbian, and of course lesbians couldn't get married! Even if they did, she wouldn't go to *that* wedding! So there was only Amy's wedding, and having a *lesbian couple* there would disrupt her moment to shine as mother of the bride! She begged Amy to see her side of things, saying, near tears, "but this will be *my only wedding!"* The irony here is that my mom had been married twice, and Amy didn't let her forget it. "No Mom," she said, "you had *two* weddings. This will be *my* only wedding, and they're invited." (Yeah, don't mess with my sister.)

Kate and Amy, true allies: They *got* what was going on with me; they *understood* me, *acknowledged* me, *empathized* with me. They *helped* me.

Tangina does get rid of the ghosts and also gets Carol Anne back; she delivers her legendary line, "This house is clean." And the ghosts *are* gone, but that much nastier thing that was in there with them—Tangina calls it "the Beast"—comes back and terrorizes the Freelings even *more*—at the end of that first movie and into a couple sequels. Some people like to trash talk Tangina for that, but I won't hear it. If it looks like Tangina failed, that's from the perspective of the living. Go talk to the ghosts about it, the ones she helped cross over to the other side. They made it! And thanks to Kate and Amy, so did I.

The Forest Is a Beautiful Fucking Nightmare

JOE

From 2006 to 2010, I began to have a recurring nightmare. In the dream, I'm in my parents' cabin in the Pocono Mountains in Pennsylvania, sitting in their living room with a large bay window facing the front yard. The cabin is deep in the woods: there's a little stone driveway leading to a dirt road, and the yard is nothing more than trees, leaves, moss, and patchy grass. It's dark, it's night, and I can see the shapes of the trees but can't see more than maybe thirty feet in front of the window; I know this house, this yard so well, but they still seemed so strange to me.

To my horror, shapes begin to pull themselves out of the ground. Human shapes, but somehow also plants. They wear suits and skirts made from leaves, and feathers in their hair. Long, rootlet tendrils fall off their bodies like leather fringe. These plant people rise from the ground, pull themselves out of trees, drop down from the leaf canopy. Some are so tangled in vines in the trees that they stay suspended, reaching their hands out towards the house. As I watch in terror, a dark, glittering purple mist follows them. Where their bodies had pulled out of the dirt and trees, so the mist pours out after them. They amass around the house, and the mist fills in around their legs and feet, so thick I can no longer see the forest floor beneath. I'm terrified, but entranced: why is this horror so beautiful? Before anything more can happen—before they get to the house—I wake up.

I really pondered my dream, trying to interpret it, and the more I read it (to filth, jk jk), the more I began to think about Darren Aronofsky's 2010 psychological thriller *Black Swan*, a movie based on the ballet *Swan Lake.* In the movie, we follow Nina Sayers, a New York Ballet Company dancer who lives in an apartment with her controlling and emotionally abusive mother. As she auditions for the lead in *Swan Lake,* she gets caught up in a world previously unknown to her, one in which she at one moment is fending off sexual advances from the play's director and the next is coaxed into trying ecstasy with her new protégé—all the while feeling an ever-growing unhinged power to revolt against her mother and the strict house that she runs. One of the ways in which Nina rebels is through an ever-present shadow self, a dark version of her—the black swan to her white—that she fears might actually be behind some of the strange things that have been happening in her life.

Soon, Nina can't quite distinguish between her real life and her hallucinations, and importantly, she can no longer distinguish between who and what she desires. Her own shadow grows stronger, spending more time directing her life for her—to her own detriment—as Nina spirals further into self-harm and paranoia. In her desire to be the lead, to play both the White and the Black Swan, Nina envisions a sexual relationship with one of her fellow dancers, one she fears is trying to take her role, and the vision is so strong that she's unsure if it really happened or not. In turn, we begin to question just what it is that's haunting her. Is it her desire to be the star, the most important dancer on the stage? Her need for freedom from her overbearing mother? A latent sexuality that she's too emotionally traumatized to have even consciously considered? Or is it all of the above? Unfortunately for Nina, we don't get to see her safely out of the woods: the creatures get to the house before she wakes up, and she never really gets to understand who they were, and what they wanted.

I've spent a lot of time thinking about my dream. Does this ever happen to you? I've had dozens of dreams that I remember, many that I can actively recall right now, but I never think about them aside from thinking, *lol, that was so weird.* But something about this dream haunts me. I've read this dream a lot of different ways: was I so stuck at home after college that I felt I couldn't leave my parents' house for fear of the monsters outside? Was I a child, safely at home, while the complicated world of adulthood was ever encroaching? Was my psyche trying to tell me I was trapped in an abusive relationship with my girlfriend-at-the-time, a person who regularly threatened to harm herself if I didn't do what she wanted and who actively worked to isolate me from my friends and family? Or was I just overthinking a dream that seemed to make more sense than my dreams usually do?

Lately, I've been thinking about how *gay* this dream was, particularly at that time in my life. My college years were a time of lots of introspection and exploration, figuring myself out and parsing out my own desires. The monsters in the dream seem different to me now than they were back then: they're beautiful and terrifying, and they represent something so deeply entrenched it had to literally pull itself from the ground—letting the prettiest, glittering mist pour out as it did. This dream is horror drag, I've decided: it *looks* scary, but I don't think it's supposed to *be* scary. It's *Dark Crystal* meets *The Boulet Brothers' Dragula.* It's the dark guardians of the forest meets Rio Carnival.

The Scandinavian *lyktgubbe*, a charming and phosphorescent will-o'-the-wisp luring me outside, no, not to my death but to a goth synthpop New Year's party with a floor full of balloons. It's night and darkness and glitter and pomp and it's all. a. bout. me. It's my fabulous shadow self coming for me.

It seems like we—both Nina from *Black Swan* and I—were going through periods of repression. A big part of my coming out was through a lot of informative discussion with my therapist, who told me that when we repress one part of ourselves, a lot of other parts get pulled down with it. Kind of like a trampoline, when you jump down on it, the whole trampoline pulls down towards the center. My queerness may have been the precious cargo I'd stuck at the bottom, but there are a lot of things I feel more confident about since coming out: I don't know exactly why, but before I came out I wasn't allowed to enjoy pop music, or think too much about how I dressed, or let go of material things. It wasn't an emotionally abusive mother I was living with, like Nina, but it was instead a thousand micro (and macro) abuses that have lived forever in my mind since I was old enough to file them away, memory by memory. But as I became more comfortable with myself, more accepting of myself, those fears just . . . released.

Nina didn't make it, but Nina was a character in a movie. Maybe, the next time I have that dream, I should open the door, step out into the glittering purple mist, and get to know my shadows—my black swans—a little better.

The Jessica Cabin

JOE

What would you do if you woke up dead one day and found that you were stuck within the confines of the physical place where you died? How would you fill your time? That's the question at the forefront of *The Jessica Cabin*, a queer ghost comedy from Daniel Montgomery. Spirit besties Jackson and Taylor watch visitors as they come and go from the rental property in which they reside, seemingly indefinitely.

How do they fill their days, you may ask? By telling stories, remembering their favorite meals from when they were alive, and obsessively following the tenants around the cabin. On one hand, it's the kind of fly-on-the-wall perspective I've long dreamed I could have in day-to-day life, but on the other, it'd be a hellishly boring life to live for . . . well, forever. While the visitors can't see them, the two certainly get the most that they can out of their occasional roommates. They follow them from room to room and play spectator to all their activities, as—ahem—*private* as some of those activities are meant to be.

But a "terrible mistake" shakes up the ghosts' seemingly everlasting afterlife, when they decide to meddle in the lives of two particularly attractive guests, Nicky and Preston. (The true star of the movie is the outfit Preston wears during their second dinner at the cabin.) Though they are ghosts and can't interact with the world around them like we can, Taylor and Jackson can perform some classic haunted house gags, such as moving and hiding things from their living guests and calling their names quietly from the other room—not scaring the people so much as trying to connect with them. But with Nicky and Preston, they take their haunting too far out of a selfish desire to shake up their own undeath. Soon our ghostly pals find themselves mired in the enormity of their actions and the weight of consequence.

The initial premise is funny enough, and *The Jessica Cabin* has comedy in spades. I could spend all day with the *dead*pan delivery (pun intended) of Riley Rose Critchlow as genderqueer spirit, Taylor, and the frankly hilarious expressions that director/writer/actor Daniel Montgomery gives his gay ghost, Jackson. There's enough chemistry between the two to warrant a reality show in which they simply follow people around making commentary of everyday life. But comedy's not the only thing *The Jessica Cabin* has packed in its bags. I teared up a few times at the confessional dialogue and the tender moments shared between the ghosts and related to the true message of the movie: is the queer experience that of being unseen? Are we simply walking among the living normies, trying to find an afterlife in which we too can just "be normal"? It's a sad, chilling thought, but one that's all too familiar to me.

There are a lot of different ways to be queer and a lot of different ways to come out. One of the things I appreciate most about the queer family I'm building in my life is the pure acceptance and joy we take in each others' coming out stories. One of the determining factors in keeping me in the closet for so long was a real feeling of imposter syndrome. I haven't had a deep relationship with a man, and I spent decades literally *avoiding* thinking about my own gender or sexual feelings. I truly believed that the only way to be gay was to be in a same-sex relationship. A mix of my Catholic upbringing and a very 1990s refusal to accept bisexuality taught me that. I shut a lot of my own feelings out when they came up because I was afraid. I chastised myself every time I watched gay pornography (but still did it, of course) and berated myself when I found a man, genderqueer person, or otherwise-non-cis female person attractive. I convinced myself that anyone could find anyone attractive, but I wasn't allowed to do so. Other people were allowed to have complicated genders, to be in a stage of exploration, questioning, and acceptance, but not me. I was just straight, that's it. My feelings were just foibles, I mean, who would accept them if I couldn't accept them myself?

The problem was I didn't know *how to listen.* I was being haunted by my own queerness. I was Jackson, only instead of watching a hunky home renter, I was watching my own body go through the motions and feeling terribly lonely. Queer me bubbled up once in a while to let myself know, *Hey, I'm here. You can't ignore me forever.* Cracks began to form in the stone-solid rules that had been set in my mind since childhood, though, and for that I have to thank my friends, and more than anyone else, my beautiful partner Katie. Some of my friends, who I really love and I know really love me, have had wildly different stories about coming out: some knew they were gay since childhood. Some came out once they were in college. Some didn't have any relationships at all until they were adults and fully understood and accepted more about themselves, the kind of understanding they needed to gain before truly accepting anyone else into their lives. Some have a fluidity that they haven't felt the need to define—at least, not to me. To be honest, I never felt straight, but I never really felt gay, either. What I often felt like was a loser. Like I didn't belong in either camp. I felt so incredibly judged by all sides. I was too straight to be gay. I'd never had a real conversation with anyone in my life about my feelings until I met Katie. The more we talked about our feelings, the more we understood about each other: we were, at the time, two straight people admitting to each other that we weren't all that straight in our most private thoughts, in our own minds. Our once-straight-facing relationship changed the more we found we were looking for the same thing. We had to step off the porch together (watch the movie, you'll get it). Sometimes I just think about how lucky I am to have found her, to have found someone who was questioning in the same way that I am. Someone to grow with and explore what our identities can mean, together. To borrow a line from a poem in her book *Spiritbox*, "Queer as in a question you never stop asking."

The Jessica Cabin is a movie that gives a lot and asks very little. By that I mean it asks questions *with* us, not *for* us. To dive too deeply into the plot of *The Jessica Cabin* is to give too much of the story away, a story that unfolds beautifully and effortlessly. While the entire film is shot at one location, it never feels claustrophobic: the characters bring such life to the cabin that we're forever inhabiting it with them, comforted by their presence. It tells us that in life we *should* do the hard work to heal, because our past traumas might follow us into death. But even in death, we learn, it's still not too late to gain a little clarity, understanding, and self-love. Hopefully we can find some of that self-love before then, but it's a beautiful thought to ponder that, even after death, we never have to give up on ourselves.

The Pact

GINA

Every time I've moved into a house, I've felt like I'm entering into a pact with something a *lot* bigger and more powerful than me and really hoping it goes okay. "Look," I want to say, "you need me to keep you up, and I need you for shelter, so can we just show some mutual respect here?" Almost always, I've been able to get along with my houses, but it's usually a bit of a process for us to get to know each other.

Every house is haunted when you first move into it. That may not be *literally* true, but does it matter? When you hear strange, unexplainable noises; when that one kitchen drawer always opens by itself; when you can't figure out where the draft in the hallway is coming from; when the corner of the basement has a puddle of water even though it hasn't rained, the plumber has checked all the pipes, and you know for sure it isn't cat pee: does it really matter whether or not the house is *literally* haunted? The house isn't keeping up its end of the pact. I've found that attention, care, and patience can win a house over. And if all this sounds demented to you, bear in mind that last sentence is also just plain good home stewardship advice, whether you rent or own, whether you live in a house or an apartment. I've eventually had good relationships with almost every house I've lived in, but here's the story of my scariest moment negotiating those early days getting to know a new house.

My partner Ellen and I had just moved in together. We rented a cute little bungalow built in 1931 that had been rented by just one other person, a nice woman with a pet iguana, and then before that, had been in the hands of the original owner, "ol' Mrs. Pohling," whom the neighbors still talked about fondly. In the end, I loved this house so much that, when we moved out, I was so sad that I cried openly in the street. But when we moved in, it wasn't really holding up its end of the pact. One room was way hotter than the others, none of the windows would open, and there was some sort of film peeling up off every floor in the whole house. Then, one night Ellen went to bed before me while I stayed up to unpack a bit more. When I finally got to bed, she sat up, looked right at me, and said, "Well, I guess now's as good a time as any to break the short shelf."

I had *no idea* what she was talking about. I sat there, looking into her eyes, trying to figure out what the hell was going on, and quickly concluded that the house was possessing her. More exactly, I concluded that the house had managed to get inside her somehow and was trying to use her as an avatar to break the short shelf! My thoughts raced with panic: Where is the short shelf? There are a ton of built-in shelves in the basement. Is one of them short? *What* is the short shelf? *What will happen when she breaks it?* I grabbed her and started shaking her by the shoulders, and she woke up, because, as she said, it was a dream—calm down, Gina!—just a dream, plus sleep-talking! Eventually, I did calm down, but even now, nearly twenty years later, I'm still not totally convinced it was just a dream. The fact that Ellen can still remember the dream with unsettling clarity ("The short shelf was up near the ceiling and ran around the perimeter of the room," she explained to me recently) does little to reassure me.

Stanley Kubrick's *The Shining* is one big reason why. Like most people my age, I saw this movie when I was too young to process it in an emotionally healthy way—I might have been thirteen? And there's *plenty* in *The Shining* to scare anyone, but what stuck with me most was the haunted house angle. It proved formative to my thinking about houses. I know, I know: the main setting of the movie, The Overlook, is a hotel, not a house. But the family whose story we follow in the movie, the Torrances, don't live in it like a hotel; they move in to act as caretakers while the hotel is closed for the off-season, November through April. For them, it *is* a house. But it's not a home, that's for sure—the movie takes pains to show us the little boy Danny's cozy room back in the family's apartment, before they move to this strange, big place. With its stately suites and well-appointed lobbies, The Overlook is impressive, but it's not in the least bit homey. Somehow, it doesn't seem like a place for people.

Yet the irony is that the Torrances are there to *be the people* for the place. They're there to enter into the pact, specifically to keep the place up through the winter. Stuart Ullman, the hotel's general manager, explains to Danny's father Jack that, as the caretakers, they're responsible for heating different parts of the hotel in rotation, performing routine maintenance, and repairing any damage as it occurs "so that the elements can't get a foothold" in what he describes as the "fantastically cruel" winters that The Overlook endures. Basically, their job is to keep the place intact. Oh, and one more thing: The Overlook is separated from the rest of civilization by a twenty-five mile stretch of road that averages twenty feet of snow every winter. Nobody keeps it clear. The Torrances are on their own.

To say that The Overlook doesn't hold up its part of the pact by being the safe place for the people taking care of it is an understatement. It's malevolent and cunning. It lays traps for the Torrances; it makes an effort to scare them. A bar with a friendly ghostly bartender materializes for alcoholic Jack, as does a seductive woman who becomes a rotting corpse. Ghostly little girls in blue dresses appear to Danny as he Big Wheels around the halls, and a tennis ball eerily rolls up to him out of nowhere, rolled by no one he can see. A ghostly guy in a bear suit terrifies Danny's put-upon mother Wendy, and Jack chases her with an ax, goaded on by the hotel. The place is deranged, perverse, and cruel, but it does have a goal it's trying to accomplish with all these horrors. It wants to possess Danny.

Now, if you're wondering why, I say: fair question. The Overlook is chock full of other people it possesses—those girls in blue dresses, the corpse-y seductive woman, the guy in the bear suit, the ghostly bartender, and all the other ghosts in the bar while Jack drinks there; it even claims Jack. Why does it want Danny too? The main argument goes that Danny has some powerful energy the house wants, but, again, *why?* There's no reasonable answer to this question because *we're talking about a house wanting to possess a little kid.* Logic doesn't really matter. You just know it's not a good thing. Danny drools and shivers; he has visions of bloodbaths cascading out of the elevators; he grumbles, then shouts "REDRUM, REDRUM, REDRUM," which he's written with lipstick on his mom's bedroom door. (Can you see now where my brain was going with that short shelf business?) It all looks pretty bad.

Danny has to physically escape the house to get out of its grip. Spoiler alert: he's able to do it eventually, though the fantastically cruel winter Ullman talked about works against him—I won't say more about that, in case you're one of the few people who doesn't know the details of how this movie ends. But one good thing about the pact you make with a house is, if it goes bad, you can usually just leave. It may cost you money, you might lose some (or all) of your stuff, or you might have to wait it out for a bit, but like Danny, you can escape its clutches. For years, the end of *The Shining* gave me such a feeling of comfort for this very reason: It proved that there's an escape clause to the pact.

Then I stumbled upon an article online about a scene Kubrick deleted from the film after its debut—like, he sent assistants out all over the United States to physically cut it out of the movie. In this scene, the general manager of the hotel, Stuart Ullman, makes an appearance at the end of the movie. He visits Danny and Wendy, who are recuperating from their ordeal at The Overlook in the hospital. Ullman says there isn't "the slightest evidence" at the hotel of any of the horrors the Torrances experienced. He doesn't outright say it, but he implies that everything they experienced was all in their heads. All the same, though, he's very sympathetic. He insists that they come stay with him in Los Angeles for a bit (sunny beaches! no cruel winter in sight!) and says he won't take no for an answer. He starts to leave, then turns to Danny and says, "Oh, Danny. I forgot to give you this. Catch." *And then he throws a tennis ball at Danny. Yes, that tennis ball.* Sure, maybe Ullman just saw the ball at the hotel and thought Danny might like to have it. *Or maybe he's an avatar of The Overlook and has been sent to get Danny and bring him back.*

I'm glad Kubrick cut this scene out—and, though the script for the scene is available online, cut it out so completely that apparently at most only one copy of it survives. It seems like even he knew that it was too gross a violation of the pact's escape clause: When you get out, you should be safe.

This Must Be the Place: Quick Horror Recs on the Theme of Scary Places

JOE

Rift (Erlingur Thoroddsen, 2017)

Rift is a chilly and trippy Icelandic horror mystery that explores all that is left unsaid after main character Gunnar travels to a lonely cabin to find and comfort his spiraling ex Einar. While they reconnect and work through the pieces of their broken relationship, another presence—living or dead?—haunts them, always on the outside looking in. I love a sensitive thriller, and *Rift* is only made more haunting and strange by Iceland's out-of-this-world landscape: a large portion of the movie's most tense parts were filmed in a jagged lava field, where the land is torn and separated by deep crevasses. Both touching and terrifying, *Rift* is as effective in its wrenching character drama as it is in the quiet horror of desperation. The acting is excellent, and I just drank in the scenery in this one.

Spiral (Kurtis David Harder, 2019)

Spiral follows two dads and their daughter as they move to a new town—a quiet, rural place where gay people just don't live.

One of the men sees his neighbors partaking in some sort of cult behavior, and the true nature of the town soon presents itself. Spooky, slow, and full of good ambiance, *Spiral* . . . spirals . . . into an action-oriented, dreamlike ending that, frankly, I wish was given more screen time than the lengthy buildup. The slight ridiculousness of the plot keeps the film from feeling too real, which I think is a good thing. If you like feeling tense and just kinda icky, give *Spiral* a watch. But think about skipping it if you're feeling nervous about getting out of the city; this movie really revels in the terror of small-town living.

***The Haunting* (Robert Wise, 1963)**

I have an incredibly early memory of this film: I watched it in the spare bedroom of my friend Donnie's house when we were in fourth grade, and we sat on the couch and held hands because of how scary it was. I've seen it a few times since then, and I really understand the subtext better now than I did when I was ten. This movie, which is based on the Shirley Jackson novel *The Haunting of Hill House*, features a really early representation of a casual, budding lesbian relationship—frightened Eleanor takes to Theodora's bed nightly, a habit which Theodora not only doesn't mind but soon encourages—which is pretty rad! Basically, a group of people led by an eminent early paranormal researcher hole up in a gorgeous, decaying mansion to finally prove the existence of the paranormal but soon find the terrors within are getting a little too real.

***The Strings* (Ryan Glover, 2020)**

The Strings is a lovely, quiet indie movie about a musician in a time of transition. The main character Katie spends a long few weeks in a winter rental to work on her first solo album after breaking away from her band. As she attempts to create her new persona, she takes a photoshoot with a woman she fancies in a dilapidated old house. Things begin to get eerie from here, as it seems something evil from that house has followed her back to the rental. Director Ryan Glover does a nice job of letting the spirit act as the physical manifestation of Katie's internal demons (in addition to exerting its own external force), and Toronto singer-songwriter Teagan Johnston does an admirable job portraying the anxiety and pain behind Katie's decision to reimagine her identity—both as a musician and a queer person. Where the movie falters, perhaps, is in its stilted dialogue and dead-slow pace, but it caught me at a time when I needed to be quiet, and I really appreciated what it brought to the table.

Screams of a Winter Night (James L. Wilson, 1979)

COZY. That's all I can think of with this movie. A large group of early-twenty-somethings take a big ol' van up to a secluded cabin on a lake that belongs to the family of the driver (who's got a real good Stephen King vibe going on; he looks just like him!). This movie hits all the nails of cozy, seventies horror on the head: a creepy gas station full of rednecks that knocks the atmosphere off-kilter from the get-go; dark, derelict cabins; fireplaces, heavy blankets, and superb seventies fashion. Once they're at the cabin the young'ns take turns telling each other scary stories around the fireplace, and we get to see them acted out, with the movie's cast playing the stories' characters, which is a nice touch. It added another dimension to each character. We get to see them for their stereotypes (the jock, the nerd, the prude, etc.) but also get to see those stereotypes further fleshed out in each scary story. As the movie progresses, we begin to wonder: Are all the stories just that, stories? Are all the pranks just pranks? Or might some of the legends surrounding Lake Duran be . . . TRUE?!! *Screams of a Winter Night* has lots of Halloween sound effects, some decent visuals for how low-budget it was, and while it's light on scares, it's high on cozy ambience. A great watch on a cold winter's night!

Crimson Peak (Guillermo del Toro, 2015)

My partner Katie and I were really excited to see this movie. In general I like Guillermo del Toro's scary movies a lot. They're often a bit cheesy, and not terribly scary, but they're always beautiful. *Pan's Labyrinth*, *Cronos*, *Don't Be Afraid of the Dark*: they're all interesting, pretty movies that are told more like fairytales than straight horror films. And *Crimson Peak* did not disappoint in that regard. Quickly: it's Victorian times, a lady meets a fella, moves with him to his creepy castle, and it gets really ghost-y and time-to-solve-a-mystery-y. The story kept me captivated, and the atmosphere—a dilapidated castle built on a mountain of blood-red clay—is gorgeous. In fact, the visual effects might be my favorite part of the movie; the lush colors of the castle and its surrounding area made the blackness of the spirits feel so total, so definite. In classic del Toro fashion, the cinematography often overshadows the story, but that's a sacrifice you make for a beautiful landscape sometimes.

The *Amityville* Pseudo-Franchise

So, I can't really call this a "franchise" as most of the movies made under the *Amityville* title are not connected to the original movie, production company, etc. Take a movie like *The Exorcist*, for instance, which was based on a book written by the writer of the screenplay and creator of the series, so there is a claim to the title and franchise rights. All *Amityville* movies are based on an event that actually, historically happened, so no one creator can stake claim to the titled name. And thus, there is no true franchise to guide the many, many Amityville movies that have come out—and even more importantly, no sense of quality control over what's being made. But there are some real gems.

There is, of course, the absolutely terrifying The *Amityville Horror* (1979), a movie based on a book of the same title that recounted the original story: in 1974, a man kills his entire family at a house in Amityville, New York, and the family that bought the house in 1975 is terrorized by evil spirits. The story was so famous at the time that even Ed and Lorraine Warren, the famous paranormal investigators, studied the house. So if you want to get a fictionalized, overblown version of the story in horrific movie form, the 1979 movie is great. The rest are all varying degrees of terrible, but many of them are really fun because of how bad and lo-fi they are: I heartily recommend *Amityville 4: The Evil Escapes* (1989) in which the Amityville demon escapes by way of a haunted lamp that looks like a tree and begins terrorizing a family in California, and my personal favorite, *Amityville: It's About Time* (1992), in which a haunted clock from the original Amityville home opens an evil portal in a new house. The rich-guy nineties home in that movie is just wonderful to look at, and the story is really bizarre.

The Beach House (Jeff Brown, 2019)

The Beach House is an excellent piece of environmental horror, focusing on a contagion spreading from the ocean onto land and how it affects a young couple (with some requisite relationship issues) enjoying a long weekend retreat at the beach. The bones of the movie are good, and action picks up about halfway through, leading to some odd and ultimately terrifying sequences. The storyline setup is nothing short of peculiar—a daughter makes an unannounced visit to her parents' beach house with her boyfriend, only to find it's already been rented to a pair of family friends, who the daughter has no knowledge of—particularly when the family friends show up unbeknownst to the young couple, and I feel there would have been a lot more opportunities for disquieting foreshadowing if they'd gone in a slightly different direction, perhaps by introducing the family friends as one of a small group of neighbors. It felt superfluous to the story in a distracting way. All in all, *The Beach House* is a pretty quiet, slow-paced entry into a burgeoning horror genre that I like more and more with each movie watched.

A HOWL IN THE WOODS

Horror About Inhuman Monsters and Things

Coming to Terms with Unfrozen Vampires

JOE

Sometimes I annoy myself when I'm watching a movie. I have a hard time suspending my disbelief in certain areas: small incongruities jump out of the screen at me, and I'll drift off into my thoughts about them, which sometimes exit my head as a screed about what's "wrong with the movie industry," or a rumination about why a director chose to overlook certain facts when making a movie. I know it's important to live in the world of the movie, but that can be very difficult when the movie just decides to ignore things like important scientific theories and facts! The problem with my annoying tendencies—aside from irritating those I'm watching a movie with—is that I want to live uncomplicatedly in the world of a movie. I try, I really do. I recognize this as both a strength and a weakness of my mind: an avid attention to detail that keeps my own work oriented and tight but often interferes with my enjoyment of things—including the fun of making my own work! For instance, as much as I love *30 Days of Night*—the excellently exciting horror action movie in which vampires attack the Arctic town of Barrow, Alaska (now called by its Iñupiaq name, Utqiagvik), which each year enters a cycle of thirty days of darkness during the winter—and as much as the gore and thrilling action keep me enthralled, I can't stop wondering why Josh Heartthrob—oops, I mean Hartnett—has one of the only beards that grows over the course of the movie. You can literally *see* the stubble and razor burn on some of the other characters. Does his brother wake up each morning, doing all he can from his hidden vantage point, the silent attic hidey-hole where he and others have escaped the watchful eye of the vampires, to creep silently down to the home's old bathroom, fill the sink with warm water, pat his face wet, apply an appropriate amount of shaving cream, and then proceed to shave, gingerly patting his face dry before looking into the mirror to acknowledge how great he looks freshly shaved, like it's any other day? Or does the stress of a month-long vampire invasion simply force his facial hair to hibernate?

Nobody Dances Out of the Closet

GINA

Most people think of Robert Louis Stevenson's 1886 novella *Strange Case of Dr. Jekyll and Mr. Hyde* as a mad scientist story, and sure enough, it is. But it's also the story of a man trying very hard to fit in. That man is Henry Jekyll. And he's not *just* a doctor; he's an "M.D., D.C.L., L.L.D., F.R.S. & c," as the story tells us, which is a whole lot of letters to say that he's credentialed in medicine and law, and at the highest levels. He's known for his excellent taste in wine and charitable work, and he has a circle of friends who are "intelligent, reputable men." He has a "large, handsome face" and is "a tall, fine build of a man." It sounds like he would have no trouble fitting in, doesn't it?

The problem is that there's more to him than just that. In his tell-all letter that concludes *Strange Case*, Jekyll lays out just how respectable a man he is. "I was born," he says, "to a large fortune, endowed besides with excellent parts, inclined by nature to industry, fond of the respect of the wise and good among my fellow-men, and thus, as might have been supposed, with every guarantee of an honourable and distinguished future." You can just feel the *but* there, can't you? *But*, he confesses, "the worst of my faults was a certain impatient gaiety of disposition." Don't get too excited about "gaiety" there; "gay" didn't settle into regular usage as slang for homosexuals until well into the mid-twentieth century. Still, though, when Stevenson published his story, while it more explicitly denoted frivolity and a carefree quality, "gay" carried vague sexual undertones, so maybe get a little excited about "gaiety"—especially considering that surviving fragments of earlier versions of the story lean in a bit more when describing what Jekyll confesses about his otherwise respectable disposition. In one, Jekyll characterizes himself as "the slave of disgraceful pleasures," in another, "the slave of certain appetites." Why Stevenson decided to go with the vaguer language is not hard to imagine; after all, he lived and wrote during the Victorian era. When pressed about Hyde's sexuality, Stevenson insisted that Hyde "is no more sexual than any other," which strikes me as a safe enough answer but not much of a denial of anything. Reputedly, Stevenson's wife so thoroughly objected to and so harshly criticized the first (and apparently considerably more salacious) draft of *Strange Case* that Stevenson burned it in their fireplace. But even in the story as Stevenson published it, Jekyll doesn't leave the word "gaiety" to do all the work describing the other, less respectable side of himself. He talks about times he "laid aside restraint and plunged in shame" by indulging the "lower elements of my soul." And while he seems to know he should be embarrassed, even mortified, by this other side of himself, which is "more wicked, tenfold more wicked" than his good side, indulging it "braced and delighted me like wine." He revels in it.

Spoiler alert for folks who haven't read *Strange Case* or seen a film or stage version of it: I'm about to reveal the twist that shocked and riveted the story's original audience. Being a talented, brilliant doctor, Jekyll manages to concoct a potion that allows him to separate what he sees as the two opposite parts of himself: the one distinguished by virtue and the other "plunged in shame," the one who shone with industriousness and the other who was tarnished with a love of "gaiety." By drinking the potion, he becomes Mr. Hyde and can pursue his heedless, base pleasures. Then he can return to his laboratory, take the potion again, and resume life as the respectable, upright Dr. Jekyll. This is exactly how the *Strange Case* is both a mad scientist story *and* a story about a man trying hard to fit in: Jekyll finds a way to divide himself, to give life to the part of him with desires that his friends and neighbors would condemn.

Jekyll did it with a potion; I did it with space. I grew up in the 1970s and 1980s in the south suburbs of Chicago, in a working-class city the daughter of working-class parents. The college I went to was less than fifteen minutes from the hospital I was born in, the beauty shop where my mom worked, the factory where my dad worked, and the homes of both sets of my grandparents. I was an apple that hadn't fallen very far from the tree in college. But while I was at home in the very literal sense of the word, I wasn't fitting in with the other girls at school. Honestly, I wasn't even trying to. Many of them were my friends, but they went on dates with boys, snuck those boys into their parents' houses or dorm rooms at night, worried about birth control—or didn't, and had pregnancies to explain. I didn't do any of these things. I worked a variety of part-time jobs, bought myself a Jeep Wrangler with a cassette deck, and listened nonstop to Indigo Girls, though—don't laugh—I had no idea they were lesbians. I stayed focused on school and was out late only at the library. Sort of by accident, I was a "good girl"; my life was very uncomplicated.

It stayed that way until I started a master's program in Chicago—the city proper, not the suburbs—and met out queer people for the first time. If it seems weird that I didn't know any before then, consider that I was raised by people who worked hard, wanted better than what they had for their kids, and drew thick lines of propriety that they felt would help themselves and their kids advance. My school in Chicago was just an hour away from home, but it felt to me like a different world. Learning some of the new friends I was making there were queer at first surprised me, then intrigued me, then felt like a realization waiting to happen—and it was, and it did. I met a girl. We went to the lesbian bars; I was such a regular at one that if you called Leona's Restaurant and ordered a pizza in my name, they delivered it to that lesbian bar. My pizza address wasn't my permanent address; I couldn't afford rent in the city, so I still lived at home with my folks, but when I made that hour's drive into the city, I could feel a part of me that had been dormant coming to life.

Here's something that most stage and film versions of *Strange Case* get wrong about Mr. Hyde: They think he's physically a monster. He isn't. Hyde is just a man, though he's a man so different from Jekyll that characters in the story who see him and know Jekyll never suspect his tie to the doctor. Remember, Jekyll has that "large, handsome face" and is "endowed besides with excellent parts." Hyde, though: Well, nobody likes the look of him, but nobody can say precisely what it is about him that bothers them. The first character to describe Hyde for us, a Mr. Enfield, offers: "There is something wrong with his appearance; something displeasing, something downright detestable. I never saw a man I so disliked, and yet I scarce know why." Our protagonist Mr. Utterson later describes Hyde as "pale and dwarfish" with a "displeasing smile," claiming that if ever a face bore "Satan's signature," it's Hyde's. So Hyde isn't handsome, and he's endowed with questionable parts at best. Also, remember how Jekyll is described as "a tall, fine build of a man"? Hyde is puny. We got that detail when Mr. Utterson called him "dwarfish," but he's not the only one to notice; other characters describe him as "a little man" and "very small." There's a reason for that, it turns out: In that final, tell-all letter, Jekyll explains that, when he started transforming into Hyde, he was "less robust and less developed," "so much smaller, slighter, and younger than Henry Jekyll" because he had been "much less exercised." As Jekyll took the potion more and more often and let Hyde out increasingly more, he became stronger and more vigorous. Hyde was developing.

Crossing the space between the suburbs and the city, being able to claim a part of myself that I was only just discovering, allowed me to develop, too. I remember back then one of my new friends asking me what it felt like to be realizing my queerness. "It feels like finding your car keys after they've been lost forever and you've been looking everywhere," I said. The analogy was more apt than even I realized at the time: I was a commuter student, but also, essentially, a commuter queer, so my car (and by extension my car keys) were like a lifeline for me back then. I went from not really trying to fit in back at home to *really* embracing the city dyke identity I'd imprinted on. My style had always been a little androgynous, but I became less self-conscious about it. Jeans, a white v-neck tee, Doc Martens, and a very cool short-billed black cap that I wore backwards became my uniform; I got a couple tattoos and some piercings. I'm positive that my changing look singled me out at home in the suburbs, but I didn't notice. I spent more and more time in the city, cultivating my new and frankly cherished identity.

Can you feel the complications bubbling up? Right then, when I really felt *like myself*—a self I really hadn't even known was possible—in Chicago, back at home my mom started wondering where the hell I was all the time. It was a fair point: I still technically lived under her roof, but I was hardly ever there. I often spent the night in the city with my girlfriend or friends. When I wasn't with them, I spent a lot of time at school, and I worked. One night my mom called me at my girlfriend's apartment (my mom thought she was just a friend) and *really* reamed me out: Where was I all these days and nights, who was I with, what was I wrapped up in? You need to know: I loved my mom (I love her still). She made my sister and me homemade Halloween costumes, threw us totally fun birthday parties well into our teens, and took us to the beach in the summer on her days off. When my folks divorced, even though she only had part-time work, she wouldn't abide losing us, and she performed miracles to keep us all together in our house. My mom's love is fierce. So is her temper, and I feared my mom (I fear her still). She was given to saying things like, "Don't start, or I'll end it real quick," and "Straighten up and fly right," pronouncements that probably sound comical to you as you read this, but I assure you, they were *not* funny when she said them. You knew not to cross her.

Sitting on the couch at my girlfriend's apartment in Chicago, holding the phone after my mom hung up on me, I saw that I was crossing her, and I couldn't see a way not to. In that moment, I knew in my heart that becoming the me I was increasingly becoming—and that I was glad, excited to become—was somehow me crossing her. And worse, I was unwilling to undo it, even if it all could be undone somehow. Telling her the truth, explaining what was going on with me, was not an option; it was very literally not a thing I could conceive of at that time, or indeed, for years to come. So I sat there holding the phone, slowly realizing that all the time I'd spent in the city becoming what felt more and more like myself, my real self, had isolated me from home in a thousand different ways. I knew that I could get off the couch right then and drive home, but I'd never be able to get there again, not like I could before. I felt alone and completely at a loss for what to do. And then I did something that I hadn't done since I was a very small child: I sobbed. Not the slow silent trickle of a tear or two while you purse your lips for a few minutes of frustration kind of tears. It was a body-wracking cry. That girlfriend whose couch I was on, we didn't end things on good terms and haven't stayed in touch, but that night when I cried and cried and cried holding the phone, she hugged me tightly for a long time, and for that, I'll always be grateful to her.

We don't know whether or not Hyde ever cries. In fact, what he ever did when Jekyll took the potion and let him out remains a mystery. This is true except for two instances when he happens to be observed by other characters who bear back reports of him, and what they observe is unmitigated, savage violence. The first is described by Mr. Enfield, who from down the street saw Hyde accidentally collide with a small girl, harmless enough to be sure, but then the horror of the incident bloomed: Instead of stopping to help her up and make sure she was all right, Hyde "trampled calmly over the child's body and left her screaming on the ground," never even slowing. It isn't until some time later that the second incident, observed by a maidservant, occurs. Late one night, from her window, she sees one of the town's revered elderly men, Sir Danvers Carew, approach and stop Hyde as he's walking and appear to ask him a question. She watched as Hyde "seemed to listen with an ill-contained impatience," then "broke out in a great flame of anger, stamping with his foot, brandishing the cane" he was carrying. But again, the worst was yet to come: "Hyde broke out of all bounds and clubbed him to the earth. And the next moment, with ape-like fury, he was trampling his victim under foot and hailing down a storm of blows, under which the bones were audibly shattered and the body jumped upon the roadway." Of course the characters who witness this behavior, as well as all the characters who learn about it, are shocked and alarmed by it, as the story's audience is meant to be—and should be.

But I want to note something about these two incidents: They don't seem to be premeditated. It doesn't seem like Hyde set out to trample a little girl or brutally kill an old man. These aren't the shameful exploits he pursues when Jekyll lets him out; they're accidental meetings that escalate into incredible violence. These are horrific incidents, and it's tragic that these characters crossed paths with Hyde. I'm not excusing his violence, but it does seem familiar to me. *Strange Case* doesn't let us get to know Hyde very well, so who knows what he was feeling at these moments in the story? One thing *I* learned sitting on my girlfriend's couch in Chicago that night my mom called is that living a double life creates a *lot* of emotional pressure, and that pressure is liable to come out with big, big feelings—like violence, for example, or tears. That emotional pressure is its own special kind of horror, and it's driven more than a few of us out of the closet.

Another spoiler alert: I'm about to give away the end of *Strange Case*. Having grown stronger every time Jekyll lets him out by taking the potion, Hyde is eventually able to muscle Jekyll into a transformation whether the esteemed doctor wants to transform or not. Hyde is unwilling to stay inside anymore; he wants out. It becomes literally impossible for Jekyll to conceal Hyde. Because Hyde is shameful to Jekyll and reviled by the community, things end badly for them both. Hyde increasingly claims the body he and Jekyll share, but during a moment when Jekyll controls the body, he drinks a fatal poison, killing them both.

My story ends more happily than Hyde's. I didn't see the new self I discovered as any more shameful or less virtuous than who I was before. And I found a whole queer culture to welcome me—bookstores and restaurants and parades. I dated more girls, made friends with people who were themselves queer or who weren't bothered that I was, and found teachers and employers who accepted me—and eventually, my family did, too. But none of that means that the time between when I sobbed on my girlfriend's couch and the happy ending was easy.

I have a saying that I made up after my own coming out experience, maybe the only saying I've ever made up that seems abidingly true: Nobody dances out of the closet. It's never an elegant, graceful act. When you do it, you're frantic, embarrassed, panicky, or awkward (or all of those); you're uncomfortable, and you make others uncomfortable. You can plot and you can plan, you can talk to your therapist, recruit allies to help, and consider the best possible time to do it: It doesn't matter. You stumble, fall, or run frantically out because you have to—because whatever was keeping you in the closet eventually becomes less terrifying than the prospect of having to stay in there.

What Is This . . . Thing?

JOE

The last time I watched *The Thing (1982)*, I kept getting these funny flares of emotion, a rush of tears to my eyes that I didn't understand. This has been happening to me a lot lately, like when I listen to the music of Björk or Aurora, or when I watch certain reality shows, particularly those about healing and change. I've always cried easily, but something has been unlocked in the last few years, and I find my tears are a little close to the surface, and I don't always know why.

When I watched *The Thing*, I couldn't get a TV special I'd seen about the early days of the AIDS epidemic in America out of my head, which was made only more pertinent by memories of the COVID pandemic. (I'm not saying that the experience of living through the COVID-19 lockdowns was the same as experiencing the AIDS crisis, but the fear was real, and I'm fortunate enough to say this is the only global pandemic I've experienced so far.) Not knowing who "has it" and not being able to tell is terrifying. Watching close friends, family, neighbors change dramatically, seemingly right in front of your eyes: it's awful. It's almost hard now to recall how scared I felt, how dire the world felt. I think the reason John W. Campbell's story about the Thing has such a lasting power is its immediacy and flexibility in application. It's a simple message: what you see might not be what actually is. This . . . *thing* that could be any of us, could be inside of any of us, destroying us and seeking out others to do the same. It's just so fucking sad, and scary. I guess bringing up those kinds of feelings, making us feel scared—that's what horror is here to do, right?

The Thing has been terrifying audiences for nearly a century, ever since its publication in 1938 as the novella *Who Goes There?* The original story goes as follows: A group of scientists in Antarctica find a twenty-million-year-old alien frozen in the ice. They bring it back to their lab, discuss thawing it out, decide they should thaw it out, and, once thawed, it ends up not being as dead as they thought it was. The alien is parasitic in nature, and it does what parasites do, infecting the crew and effectively replicating itself in their bodies—to terrifying effect. The crew then must decide: Should they attempt to save themselves when any one of them could harbor the creature? Do they dare bring it back to the world they know, a world where it can run rampant and potentially end humanity? Each retelling and adaptation takes its own liberties, and the theme shifts with those liberties, but the story remains relatively the same.

I wanted to live in the world of *The Thing* for a few days, so I read the novella and watched the three movies. (I did not, however, read the difficult-to-find and very expensive novelization of the first movie that came out in 1982, which, interestingly, changes a number of scenes because it was written before the movie was finished. Nor did I read the various, nearly-impossible-to-track-down-and-prohibitively-expensive comic books that have come out over the years from different publishers.) Anyway, here's what I thought of everything I could get my bloody claws on!

Who Goes There? (1938)

One of the more interesting aspects of reading *Who Goes There?*, the 1938 novella written by John W. Campbell (but first published under the name Don A. Stewart in *Astounding Science Fiction* magazine) is that, at first, the story feels very modern. It was only when I started to question the actions of the characters and their equipment—you tried to break into the frozen spaceship using battery acid? Your ax was made of bronze?—that I remembered this novella is nearly one hundred years old. The dialogue eventually degrades into the speech patterns of its time, all quick jokes and complex, alien-to-me idiomatic phrases, very stage play. Some of the language is rather poetic—a remnant from Victorian writing—but not so stylistically old as to make it anything other than beautiful: The Thing is described as having a "life-smell," the surface outside the arctic station was "white death," and the "wolf-wind" howled outside. (The bisexual urge to relate everything to wolves, amirite? Just kidding, I don't think John W. Campbell was gay or anything, even if he did write a story that's a pretty good allegory for coming out, and the weird pervasive idea that gay people might "infect" "straight" people and somehow make them gay, in addition to my earlier thoughts about this story and pandemics. I don't think this is even the strongest queer theme we can find in the book, though; read on as I continue to review the series and delve deeper into its themes of toxic masculinity and forced normalcy!)

Plot-wise, the team finds this alien creature frozen in the ice and must decide: Do we thaw it and risk releasing alien microorganisms? Or do we leave it frozen and dissect it when we can do so in a more controlled environment? It's a thought that still terrifies biologists regarding climate change and the unfreezing glaciers today: *What the hell is under there? Could it still be alive?* Eventually, the Thing thaws and begins its journey, copying the men to the best of its ability in looks and infecting them bit by bit in a glorious mish-mash of horror and excellently forward-thinking sci-fi. They soon have to wonder: is this my colleague I'm speaking with or a near-perfect rendition of him played by an ancient alien? The story's trajectory is most similar to the plot of *The Thing* (1982) than any of the other interpretations, and it's pretty damn scary.

PS: Best line in the book: "Damn it, I missed that moon cut in the door he carried out more'n I missed the sun when it set." If you had any doubts this was written in the thirties, there's your proof: an outhouse in Antarctica!

PPS: The next time someone seems like they've stopped paying attention when I'm talking, I'm going to do what McReady does: when he sees the vacant looks on his colleagues' faces during one of his speeches, he says, "Having a lovely time. Wish you were here. Signed: Everybody." Such a power move.

Frozen Hell (1938/2019)

In the preface to *Frozen Hell*, writer Alec Nevala-Lee tells an anecdote about John W. Campbell: While working through various versions of *Who Goes There?*, he talked with a chemist friend who introduced an interesting problem in the science community at the time, which was, if we were to discover alien life, would we be able to determine if it were a plant or an animal? Or would it be both, or something different entirely? Campbell liked this idea so much that it became the major plot point for *Who Goes There?*, and eventually, *The Thing*.

The major difference between *Who Goes There?*, the version published serially in *Astounding Science Fiction* Magazine, and *Frozen Hell*, the fuller version Campbell originally wrote for publication, is a lengthy three-chapter opening that was rewritten again and again, each time from a different character's perspective before being finalized from the vantage point of McReady, the protagonist of the story.

Frozen Hell is a little lackluster in its presentation, whereas *Who Goes There?* is tight, terrifying, dramatic. *Frozen Hell* is a thoughtful, cheerful, and interesting story about scientists in the Antarctic, but it basically presents two stories: the adventures of the scientists discovering—and inadvertently destroying—a spaceship in the ice, while also discovering the frozen being—replete with some dated rat-a-tat-tat dialogue—followed by a few lectures and loads of scientific information, and THEN followed by the same tight, terrifying, dramatic story. Campbell himself took his editors seriously, learning a valuable lesson about starting a story the right way and determining that the first three chapters weren't necessary to start the story of *Who Goes There?* right. While *Frozen Hell* is an interesting artifact, I wouldn't recommend it as a read for those only lightly interested in where the Thing comes from.

Perhaps the most interesting revelation in *Frozen Hell* comes in the introduction from science fiction author Robert Silverberg. He tells us that John Campbell's mother had an identical twin, a woman who had a contentious relationship with his mother and who he often couldn't tell was *not* his mother. So little John might come home upset from a bad day at school and be met with cold apathy from his mother, only to find it was his aunt. It's hard to separate this anecdote from the monstrous mimicry of the Thing!

It's an intensely interesting idea for the context of our book, too: we queer people spend a lot of time relating to the monster, but sometimes the monster is *not* us: it's the fucked up world we live in. In this case, the Thing actually *is* a monster! It's true that it has a really hard time blending in, but not because it wants to be accepted and can't be, and not because the external pressure on it to conform is too much to bear. In all instances of the story, the Thing stands for destruction, death, and hatred. It's completely outside of us, an external force that appears friendly but attempts to destroy the human race, and on a deeper level, one of the very things that makes us human: our ability to connect with each other without causing harm. This Thing, this terrible, awful Thing, is toxic masculinity. It's patriarchy, it's capitalism, it's presidents and dictators and autocrats who sow discord and distrust for their own selfish needs. It's the false friend who tells you they care and then use what little power they have to elect the Thing into office. It's anyone who sees another person as lesser-than. It's more apparent in *Frozen Hell* than in most of the reinterpretations that the Thing here truly is a monster.

PS: In this edition of my secret gameshow *Is It Gay Lingo or Just Really Dated*, one of the more comical aspects of *Frozen Hell* is that the men keep calling each other "you birds," which later came to be used as a slightly rude British term to describe young women. When asked if they could store the frozen alien in the meat freezer, the chef replies, "Hey, you listen mister, you put that thing in the box with the meat, and by all the gods that ever were, I'll put you in to keep it company. You birds have brought everything you could think of in on my tables here already . . ." Green's Dictionary of Slang informs me that the word has on and off over the centuries also been used to refer to men, sort of like you'd use the word "guy." But it's still funny to me in a modern genderplay kind of way to think of these tough arctic scientists calling each other "birds."

The Thing from Another World (1951)

The Thing from Another World is a classic. Like, a legitimate classic that set up the cinematic crossroads of horror and sci-fi for decades to come. It's not exactly scary, and it hardly lends itself to good, queer analysis, but it did a lot of things right: you don't often see the monster (which usually makes the monster scarier—your imagination creates the beast!), the seeds of distrust sewn among the characters create a chilling atmosphere, and the monster, when it does appear, is at once both alien and disturbingly human, and much more plant-based. It first seems to gravitate around the station's greenhouse. Since this movie deviates a little from the original novella in order to make a more heavy-handed moralistic comment on society and the blind faith we put in science (ah, the fifties), watching it makes me appreciate just how loyal *The Thing* (1982) was to the original story, while adding in extra elements of horror to its sci-fi core.

One thing I will say, though, is that this movie is old—and feels it. In life's great pantheon of things to watch, read, do, listen to, and all the various other ways to entertain yourself, I'm okay with letting you know that, hey, you don't have to watch this movie. Like the novella, the dialogue is spoken almost too quickly and sounds goofy for it, like a stage play; the women are largely there to be looked at and commented on; and there is an incredibly awful racist joke. *Woof.* You could probably skip this addition to the franchise if you don't feel like dealing with that, or take it with a heaping of salt. I feel I can confidently say you're never going to find yourself saying, *Wow, in everything I did in life, I can't believe I never watched 1951's The Thing from Another World.*

What I love best about this movie is my memory of watching it on the couch with my dad when I was really, really little, like five or six years old. I was that kid who just LOVED bugs, and aliens, and Lego sets, and inventing worlds to live in and stuff. This movie was one of my dad's favorites when *he* was a kid, and when he and I watched old sci-fi movies together, it didn't really feel like *dad and son* anymore. It felt more like two friends, sitting under blankets, hiding their eyes from the scary parts.

Horror Express (1972)

I'm going to make a statement, and it's going to be definitive but with the caveat that I understand that I'm saying it for and about myself, and that the statement is open to much disagreement, based entirely on personal opinion: bad horror movies are the coziest movies around. They were made to be watched either on a very hot day, when you've just come in from yard work and your brain has basically fried (pun intended, read on!) or on a very cold day, when you've decided to shirk all responsibility and just exist for a little while, basically napping with your eyes open—or closed. Maybe it's not even fair to make this determination. There are all kinds of bad movies, and this isn't actually even a bad movie, it's just old and a little dry.

There's a lot to recommend *Horror Express* re: coziness. The warm grain of the film. The dark, shadowy lighting that persists throughout most of the scenes. The monster-movie scares that are more akin to a film from 1962 than 1972. But! The monster! Oh, the monster is pretty rad. It draws heavy inspiration from the ideas in Campell's original novella, even though this story is not connected to any of the creators. Something of a pre-human mummified sorcerer, it seems. Maybe it's a primitive energy vampire? That's also a slimy, hairy, magical zombie? Then, through some trick of science that must have existed in 1906 (when this movie takes place), they determine it to be an alien creature that takes over people's bodies (either that or, ya know, god). It seems to boil the brains of its victims until their eyes turn white and blood drips from their eyes and mouths. It's not as gross as it sounds. I dig it.

In my own mythos, within *The Thing* universe, this story is about the alien being transported down from the arctic station: they hint at this in *Horror Express* but never directly reference *The Thing* or any of Campbell's work. Fun fact: you can see much of this movie in an episode of *Creepshow*, in the excellent reboot of the series that's on Shudder. Second season, fifth episode, the one where the guy invents a machine that lets him insert himself into movies. This is one of the movies he was obsessed with, and he gets all flirty with one of the ladies on the train.

Anyway. *Horror Express* isn't the most exciting movie you'll ever see in your life, but I enjoyed it. It's a good movie to watch on the kind of day when you feel a little sleepy and are considering a quick snooze on the couch, but want to more or less watch a movie.

The Thing (1982)

The Thing (1982) is one of the greatest horror / sci-fi crossovers in all of not just horror movie history but movie history altogether. I think one of the greatest achievements of the film was investing so heavily in special effects and monster makeup. One of, ahem, the things about the Thing is that it infects living organisms like a virus, then genetically copies them, but it gets a little mixed up at first. So the first few monsters you see are kind of like the original animal or person, but they usually have some . . . added features that that animal or person might not have in the first place. Because of this, the creatures that the Thing inhabits are really the stuff of nightmares. Ever seen a dog with a giant snaking human neck and head attached? The film features some of the wildest, most terrifying scenes I've ever witnessed, scenes that haunt me (probably because I was like ten when I watched this for the first time).

The Thing is grotesque, and it's hard not to watch this movie and see an allegory for illness and infection. A lot has been said about the theme of distrust, but I feel the movie is rife with commentary on the theme of infection: how does sickness, mental or physical, change us? How quickly can we recognize those changes and get to safety before we, too, get sick? Far too often in the movie we see characters cosying up to the Thing, not realizing how imminent the danger of their own infection is.

But what *is* the infection? What is the Thing today, in 2025? For too long the queer community has seen itself as the monster—and I get it, I really do, we even draw the same conclusion a few times in this book. Sometimes we are! The monster is a complicated concept. But how wonderful would it be to look at the Thing and realize that this monster has no redeemable qualities: this isn't the monster you want to love, the monster who is only a monster because she's shunned from everyday society. This is a new monster that's all-too-real today, a monster that infects peoples' minds. It's the monster you can't see but that lashes out when you're weak. It's the monster that seethes when you relate your pronouns at a work meeting, the monster that crosses your name off the list when it, your "friend," finds out you're gay. This monster waits until you're at the holiday dinner table and knows you're too polite to cause a ruckus, so it rails against you and people like you, making snide comments then hiding behind the retort, "Can't you take a joke?" It's the social media comment your friend or relative makes that they think you won't see. The monster isn't me, this time: this is a monster of intolerance, of hate, and not the internal kind. The Thing lashes out to kill others and we never get to know why. Sometimes the best course of action is to realize that, no, I'm not the monster, and I never was. Sometimes you have to kill the monster. And if you can't kill it, you just have to get as far away from it as you can.

The Thing (2011)

The latest iteration of *The Thing* is a needless addition to the franchise that acts as both a prequel to the 1982 masterpiece and a kind of remake of that same movie. You may recall that the 1982 version begins with two Norwegian men in a helicopter hunting an escaped husky, both men eventually dying in the chaos of the hunt while the dog finds the American base. *The Thing* (2011) tells the story of the Norwegian base and the events leading up to that scene. Somehow, a movie about Norwegian scientists still manages to find a way to make (different) Americans the heroes, which I found to be an odd choice.

What we have here is a limp prequel to the 1982 movie that, while it does boast a few exciting scenes, will have a great legacy as . . . a link on the Wikipedia page for *The Thing* (1982), which you open when reading about the original movie, then close a few minutes later without reading once you reach the *what-even-am-I-doing* point of going down a rabbit hole about one movie. It offers no new perspective and spends a great deal of time watering down the themes of the original work.

A Stroll Through "Goblin Market"

GINA

In 1996, I was twenty-four years old and working on my master's degree in English literature at a university in Chicago. I was in a Victorian poetry class with, and friends with, the first three out queer people I'd ever known in my life, plus quickly realizing that I am myself a lesbian. It was for that class that I read "Goblin Market" for the first time.

The English poet Christina Rossetti published the poem "Goblin Market" in 1862. It tells the story of two innocent maidens who tangle with goblin merchants peddling poisoned fruit, so it's a page-turner even just from a narrative perspective, plus many scholars have offered compelling interpretations of the poem as being about religion, capitalism, tainted food in the Victorian marketplace, addiction, and even the production of art. I have taught this poem in my own classes many times, and if I put on my English teacher hat, I could explain the finer points of any and all of these interpretations. But I still can't decide what "Goblin Market" says about the one theme it engages that meant the most to me when I first encountered it back when I was twenty-four years old: the theme of lesbian desire.

Most certainly, critics have recognized this theme of the poem, too—it's kinda hard not to. I mean, just look at the original cover illustration for the book that contained the poem.

Those women enveloped in an intimate embrace are Laura and Lizzie, the two innocent maidens whose story the poem follows, as drawn by Christina Rossetti's brother, Dante Gabriel Rossetti. It's not like he took a ton of liberties imagining our protagonists for this drawing, either; indeed, at one point early in the poem, Rossetti describes Laura and Lizzie sleeping

> Cheek to cheek and breast to breast
>
> Locked together in one nest.

How could this be a poem about anything *other* than lesbian desire—and a very sweet poem at that? Well, buckle in, and heads-up: spoilers ahead.

The poem opens with Laura and Lizzie out one evening as the sun sets. They hear the hawking cries of approaching goblin merchant men, presented by the poem as a regular feature of their world:

Morning and evening
Maids heard the goblins cry,
"Come buy our orchard fruits,
Come buy, come buy!"

The goblins are never intricately described but are called "little men" and characterized by a welter of animal words—they are "Cat-like and rat-like, / Ratel- and wombat-like" and "Chattering like magpies, / Fluttering like pigeons, / Gliding like fishes"—suggesting they're hybrids, if not in appearance, at least in demeanor.

Catching their calls on the wind, Lizzie rehearses what sounds like the "old wisdom" of the poem's world:

We must not look at goblin men,
We must not buy their fruits;
Who knows upon what soil they fed
Their hungry thirsty roots?

But Laura—stupid Laura!—looks, lingers, and wants a taste. But, oh no! She has no money to pay the goblins! Not a problem, they say; pay us with a lock of your hair. *This is a bad sign.* I think we'd all be smarter than to ever pay for anything with a lock of our own hair; it's an arrangement with *dirty business* written all over it. But of course Laura does, and then indulges herself with their fruits. But for real:

[She] suck'd their fruit globes fair or red:
Sweeter than honey from the rock,

Stronger than man-rejoicing wine,
Clearer than water flow'd that juice;
She never tasted such before,
How should it cloy with length of use?
She suck'd and suck'd and suck'd the more
Fruits which that unknown orchard bore;
She suck'd until her lips were sore. . . .

So: yeah.

Laura walks home in the gloaming to find a worried Lizzie, who chides her with one of my favorite lines of the poem: "Twilight is not good for maidens." And look, if it's your first time through the poem, it's easy to see Lizzie as a total wowser and pooh-pooh her along with Laura, who's like, "*Puh-lease!* I had a great time, and OMG I can't wait for you to taste that fruit!" But then, Lizzie reminds Laura of another maiden, Jeannie, who also ate with the goblins—once and only once—and paid a heavy price for it, because she could never hear nor see them again, and

She pined and pined away;
Sought them by night and day,
Found them no more, but dwindled and grew grey;
Then fell with the first snow,
While to this day no grass will grow
Where she lies low:
I planted daisies there a year ago
That never blow.

Laura responds, essentially, "Yeah, yeah; you'll see." But Lizzie winds up being right; Laura can't hear the goblins' "fruit-call," as the poem terms it, and she goes into hardcore goblin fruit withdrawal: she "gnash'd her teeth for baulk'd desire, and wept / As if her heart would break." She grows weak, thin, and pale.

Beside herself with worry, Lizzie decides to go find the goblin men and do a takeout order for Laura. This *reeeeeaaaaaalllly* peeves the goblins, who get so mad that she won't eat with them that they assault her with their fruit, pelting her with it and smashing it into her body so that she's positively dripping with goblin fruit, and they seem to feel like *they sure showed her.* But then Lizzie goes back to poor, jonesing Laura and presents her goblin-fruit soaked self, urging her:

> Hug me, kiss me, suck my juices
> Squeez'd from goblin fruits for you,
> Goblin pulp and goblin dew.
> Eat me, drink me, love me;
> Laura, make much of me. . . .

So, again: yeah.

Laura does suck her juices, and gets *hella* sick—apparently goblin fruit the second time you have it is particularly strong medicine but a potent antidote to the first taste of goblin fruit and the intense craving it creates. She survives, recovers her health, and is so, so grateful to Lizzie. And then the poem winds up in what has always seemed to me a very weird way: Laura and Lizzie become "wives / With children of their own." Yeah, you read that right: *wives.* With *children.* But they hang out together and gather the kids round to tell them tales of

> The wicked, quaint fruit-merchant men,
> Their fruits like honey to the throat
> But poison in the blood;
> (Men sell not such in any town)

And Laura in particular

Would tell them how her sister stood
In deadly peril to do her good,
And win the fiery antidote.

If this was not the ending you saw coming for the two birds locked together in one nest, *you're not alone.* That's part of where all my confusion about this poem came from in 1996, and frankly, still comes from today.

But let's back up a couple steps: Where's the horror in this poem? It's easy to lose track of it in the fairy tale ending. Of course, our antagonists, the goblin merchant men, with their hybrid bodies, ill-intentioned behaviors, and poisoned fruit, are the main external source of horror in the poem. But I'd say even more potent is the internal horror of the maidens' yearning for the goblin fruit; it makes them unsafe in their own world—indeed, not safe from themselves. Given these two elements of the poem, one way to think about what this poem presents as horrifying is that it's women *having* to have sex with men: the goblins are, after all, merchant *men,* out there peddling their wares, creating desire that women, *some* women, anyway, having had a taste, apparently just cannot sate.

So then, is the release from this horror for women to have sex instead with women? You don't have to read too much into the poem to see that Laura's feast with the goblins was . . . kinda sexual, and her interaction with the fruit-soaked Lizzie was . . . ditto. So lesbian sex saves the day? That would be a great moral, but it isn't what the poem actually says. I mean, consider that Lizzie is only attractive to Laura when she's covered in goblin juices—we could say, when she's in goblin drag. And once Laura recovers from the whole goblin misadventure, she's maybe not interested in Lizzie in that way anymore: She gets married, has some kids.

And while we're on the topic of marriage: why isn't sex with a husband—sex that presumably produced those kids—poison to Laura, or Lizzie for that matter? Presumably because their husbands aren't themselves goblins, aren't those funny hybrid men. So the poem might be suggesting that the goblins represent desire that's sinister, deviant, something you only do in the dark. In short, the goblins might best be read as queer: *that's* what makes them dangerous.

If that's right, then I think "Goblin Market," despite its fantastic cover and even racy Laura-Lizzie feeding scene, fails to be a lesbian poem. In fact, it may go so far as to disavow lesbians silently as it explicitly condemns the goblins for their queerness, which is perhaps to be expected for a poem written in Victorian England. But even as it uses the goblins to preach the dangers of queer desire, the poem reveals its strong pull. Sure, Laura's sister dragged her back to the *straight* and narrow path, but I bet she still turned her ear to the window above her kitchen sink and tried to catch the goblins' call while she did the dishes after dinner.

Of course, one potential problem with this tidy interpretation is that the poem doesn't say Laura and Lizzie have husbands. It says they're *wives*, with children of their own. (The poem also uses the word "sisters" to refer to them, but I've always read this as a term of camaraderie rather than familial relation.) In Rossetti's time, that implied husbands; it wasn't a regular thing then for a couple of wives to have children together. But it is today. So, then, possibly, if you read it through a modern lens, this can be a lesbian poem, lesbian sex *did* save the day, and goblins represent all men, who are all dangerous. But even in this reading of the poem, Lizzie has to douse herself in goblin juice to get Laura to notice her. And that reminds me of benighted straight old people who ask lesbian couples, “Which one of you is the man?” In short, it’s not the best way to write a lesbian romance. Also, I’m really not a fan of separating a poem from the historical context in which it was written—I think it unmoors the poem and leads to a sort of interpretative free-for-all.

The truth is, nearly three decades of reading “Goblin Market” hasn’t gotten me any closer to feeling like I understand its ultimate message. I think one reason the poem has continued to be so important for me is because of this, because I can’t figure out what it’s saying about lesbians. I have a feeling that whatever it’s saying isn’t good, but I love this poem and want it to do right by lesbians. That’s probably too much to ask of a Victorian poem. Still, though: more than a few of Rossetti’s verses, and certainly her brother’s illustrations of the poem, insinuate that there are more possibilities for the maidens in this poem than its ending describes, and that’s gotta count for something.

I Am the Lamb, the Lamb Is I

JOE

Have you seen *Lamb,* the 2021 A24 folk horror film? This disquieting movie was co-written by director Valdimar Jóhannsson and the incredible Icelandic author/punk/poet Sjón. It's a great piece of gentle, slow-burn horror about a childless couple, María and Ingvar, living on an Icelandic sheep farm, who find a child on their land. This child, Ada, comes to them through truly odd—and disturbing—means, but the couple comes to love her and accepts her as their own.

The movie adds other delicate and intricate layers, weaving themes of childlessness, loneliness, adoption vs. birth, and man vs. nature throughout, and creating one of the most blatant are-we-the-monster allegories I've seen in awhile.

There are a lot of possible readings of the film. One of the most compelling, I think, is the idea of man vs. nature: namely, can we ever truly be a part of the natural world and come to love it as much as we love ourselves, or will there always be an inherent disconnect between us and nature because of the human ego? Wild stuff to think about.

But that isn't the reading I want to talk about, nor is it the one that came to me during the first, or even second, time I watched *Lamb;* no, it's hard for me to see past the film as an allegory for the difficulty a family can have with accepting a queer child.

Ada is born, not to María and Ingvar but on their farm and is taken by the couple and reared as their own. Her new mother shows her nothing but infinite love, while her new father takes a little longer to accept her as a part of his family. The little family unit eventually gels, but that peace is badly shaken when Ingvar's wayward brother Pétur comes calling for a place to stay. The way her uncle regards her stung for me, reminded me of some of the little tête-à-têtes I've had with some adults through the years, when I was much younger, the homophobic comments they made when we were alone, always with a face of anger and hatred hidden behind a terrible smile. The kind of people who are the epitome of *can't you take a joke.* I like to call this "preventative homophobia," the idea that by lashing out and attacking queer culture, adults can stymie any burgeoning feelings in the youth around them, particularly in family members. Back then I wasn't even out yet, but the bullies are always the first ones to know.

I had the good fortune of meeting Sjón, the co-author of *Lamb*, at an art book fair in Reykjavík, Iceland, and we had a lovely conversation in which he spoke to the open-ended nature of the interpretation of the movie. While he didn't intend for the movie to be an allegory for queer youth, he was quite pleased with that reading and mused about the many messages a single movie can hold, so many unique to each viewer. A good film must always tell a story, he told me, and a good story can speak to many things. He recommended a piece of his nonfiction-by-way-of-historical-fiction, a book called *Moonstone: The Boy Who Never Was. Moonstone* follows Máni Steinn Karlsson, a sixteen-year-old boy who has sex with men for pay in Reykjavík in the early 1900s. Máni, a loner who is obsessed with the local cinema and the burgeoning horror film scene, and who lusts after a local tomboy who comes to represent to him a new way of life, one in which gender and sexuality are fluid and open, where he can live comfortably without judgment and scrutiny from his peers. As Reykjavík descends into a flu epidemic, Máni now finds himself living in a place that mirrors his inner self and the scary movies he's come to love so much: quiet, despairing, lonely, terrifying. He's never felt more at home.

I've long asked myself why I feel so at home among horror movies. What is it about being scared that makes me feel comfortable? Why do I find it not only entertaining, but *soothing* to give myself the willies? It's a thought that I dig into in this book, over and over again, one that I still haven't quite pinned down. I have a feeling that a few years from now, I'll be able to look back on this book and go, "Oh, THAT'S what I was exploring, now I understand I felt that way because . . ." Dang, it didn't work. I was hoping I could trick myself into answering that question right now.

Luckily, I don't *need* to answer that question conclusively right now: It's a question I'm always asking, a lifelong search for my own meaning. That's the nature of art, right? Regardless of the meaning the artist puts into the piece, the observer is always finding their own. A successful piece of art will not only encourage the viewer to see what the artist has to say, but also expand on that meaning for themselves. *Lamb* has a lot to say, and a lot of different lessons to take from it. I'm always disturbed to see reviews of movies online that not only miss the meaning I've found in a film, but seem to find no meaning in the film at all. It's fine to not like a movie—I haven't liked dozens of movies that have lots to say, lots of good points to make—I just hope for everyone to grow a little more empathy for anyone outside their own likeness. To not see the implied meaning in a film is a failure of the filmmaker, but to not take any meaning at all from the movie is a failure of the viewer. The hope, of course, is that the more media we create that paints pictures of someone outside of ourselves, someone with wholly different experiences than we have in life, the larger our kindness can grow, and our empathy. If there's one thing we can always use in this world, it's more empathy.

A Most Fearsome Beast: Quick Horror Recs on the Theme of Monsters

JOE

Trick 'r Treat (Michael Dougherty, 2007)

I watch a lot of scary movies by myself, but sometimes I'll get ten or fifteen minutes into a movie and I'll stop myself: Katie has to see this! This was one of those movies. So that night, we made a bowl of popcorn, pulled up some blankets onto the futon (ah, the futon years), and queued up *Trick 'r Treat.* WOW. I loved it, and so did she. The stories are told as an anthology of short, intertwined stories, all occurring on one Halloween night in one town, almost like a comic book in the style of *Creepshow.* Each segment is legitimately scary, and it'd be difficult for me to pick a "favorite" one, as I loved all of them. You know what? I'm not going to tell you anything more about this movie. I was *delighted* the first time I watched it, and I want you to have that experience. I bet you'll never guess what happens in the woods!

WNUF Halloween Special (Chris LaMartina, 2013)

Woah, I LOVED this movie. That doesn't mean it was the best movie I've ever seen, but I truly loved the experience of watching it. It brought me back to what it was like to watch TV as a kid, a time when I was often watching a flurry of different things all in one evening: a lurid criminal story on the news, cartoons, janky local commercials, music videos, and on and on. Sometimes I shake my head at my current phone habit, annoyed with myself for spending so much time scrolling through social media apps and news stories, then I remember that TV has trained me to zombie out and shut off my brain like that since childhood. Anyway, the storyline of *WNUF* is told like a news broadcast. The movie includes fake eighties TV commercials, reporter banter, on-the-spot reporting, ghost hunting, and much, much more! The ending was a little disappointing—it got pretty silly—but the movie is such a fun ride. It's not really actually all that scary, but that's okay. Sometimes the fun of a horror movie is in the atmosphere it creates, not the actual scares it presents. It's a spoof of the BBC's *Ghostwatch*, which in itself was a prank (more on that below). This is a watch-every-Halloween kind of movie in our household, and I hope it becomes that for you, too.

Ghostwatch (Craig William Macneill, 1992)

So this was like, totally fucked up. It was WAY scarier than a lot of the nonsense movies that are made nowadays, and it was originally created as a prank and aired on Halloween night in 1992 on the BBC. Like, if I saw this back then, when I was the age I was then (I'll never tell), staying up with my parents and all hopped up on sugar, I would have been TERRIFIED. This was everything I wanted for Halloween: this movie, with its early-nineties cheesiness and not-so-subtle nods to the famous paranormal investigators, the Warrens, is not only legitimately scary, but it's also super cozy! Basic premise: The BBC does a special on a haunted house. They send in a reporter and her team to investigate it, but it turns out that the house really *is* haunted, and they have to deal with a serious demon who's being beamed directly into the studio. Yikes! It's the BBC at its best, doing the Orson Welles sort of thing mixed with a little Enfield poltergeist. Total recommend. It's hard to find things both a little scary, and SUPER cozy, in that early nineties shot-on-film kind of way.

The Monster Club (Roy Ward Baker, 1981)

Wow, I want to go to The Monster Club with Vincent Price! This anthology of short films, tied together with a pretty silly narrative story in which Vincent Price is hanging out at a literal nightclub for monsters, was everything I wanted for Halloween. Vincent Price, here playing a vampire, meets a horror writer on the streets of London and invites him to party at his monster club, wherein the writer is told scary tales—the anthology movies—and entertained between those tales by various new wave, punk, and rock bands. The story sequences are a delightful mix of cheesy, spooky, funny, and disturbing, and the occasional club scenes are just a riot. The band performances were my favorite part of the movie. The whole thing had that excellent made-for-kids-but-kind-of-not feeling to it. It's a really safe entry to horror, and for all my babes out there who are not into gore, and really scary stuff, this movie is a fun way to spook yourself a little without having to think about it too much once bedtime rolls around.

Hell House LLC (Stephen Cognetti, 2015)

This was actually a very cool movie, but was also a little annoying. It comes and goes in waves. Basically, some young folks are setting up a hell house in an abandoned hotel and some of the props start moving on their own. Very *Five Nights at Freddy's*, and I hated it. I mean, I hated it in a good way. I felt like my heart couldn't handle it! The "documentary" part of the movie was not poorly done, but felt really unnecessary—lot's of talking heads discussing the history of the town, explaining who people were, and so on and so forth. Here the acting was at its worst, and there is little fun to be found compared to the found footage aspects. I'd go so far as to say the first twenty-five minutes of the movie *almost* made me turn it off and move on. I wanted this movie to embrace its found footage-ness and stop analyzing it with the goofy actors and townspeople and stuff. The found footage pieces were so legitimately scary! I mean, I get it. They wanted to try something new, they didn't want to just make another found footage movie. BUT THEY SHOULD HAVE! Every time my heart started racing and I felt spooked, they'd start doing that narration thing, and it really distracted me from the spookiness of the movie. In the end, though, they knew their movie, they knew the limitations of their budget, and they knew how to make a very unsettling movie using that limited budget. Total recommend—but as a note, you can generally skip the sequels.

Night of the Demons (Kevin Tenney, 1988)

This movie is totally awesome. The soundtrack is amazing—it's got music by Bauhaus and some ridiculous-yet-awesome song called "Computer Date" by the director's brother. And the usual cast of friends who would NEVER be friends in real life: a goth girl, an anarcho-punk pig, a Brooklyn tough guy, a prepster, a dork, a normie—everyone partying at once. In a sentence, a group of teen friends head to a haunted old derelict mansion to party on Halloween night, but they unleash something while there. It's some of the best teen horror that the eighties has to offer, and that's really saying something! It's cheesy, it's a little creepy, it's got super awkward sexual overtones, there are a lot of laughs, and a few jumps—it's just bananas. AND SQUIRTING EYEBALL POPPING. This is up there with my favorite movies. And the best part is, it's actually kind of scary! PS: Linnea Quigley, be still my beating heart!

Wendigo (Larry Fessenden, 2001)

Yo! I'm not going to lie, I avoided watching this movie for YEARS because I thought the cover art was so bad that I didn't want to give it the time of day. As I was watching the opening credits, only then did I see, woah! Larry Fessenden? Patricia Clarkson? This movie must be legit! *Wendigo* turned out to be a slightly janky, low-budget affair with odd sound effects, stylishly stilted scenes, and excellent performances from Clarkson, Jake Weber, and the kid from *Malcolm in the Middle.* It weaves a fairytale about the surreal wrath of nature around a very real story of the shittiness of a loserish man. Hence the name: a wendigo is a malevolent spirit from North American Algonquian-speaking people's mythology that possesses a man and fills him with greed and insatiable hungers—often cannibalism. It seems like this movie is a little polarizing; the odd, late-nineties effects and cinemagraphic choices might not be for everyone. But I liked it!

The Fog (John Carpenter, 1980)

The Fog is a sick movie. A fog rolls into a coastal town, and only too late do its residents realize that the fog brings with it an ancient, undead troop of pirates who roll in to massacre anyone stupid enough to answer the door when they knock. (They're really polite in that way. They only kill those who answer the door.) Adrienne Barbeau plays a radio DJ who is one of the first to recognize the correlation between the fog and the deaths in town, and she spurs on the people in the town to run when they can. It's some excellent old-fashioned horror, and the fog allows for the monsters to be minimally seen, making it a classic; you can't really even tell how "good" or "bad" the costumes are. Worth a watch, even if it features a number of lulls in excitement.

Cold Skin (Xavier Gens, 2017)

This is quite the movie. It's pretty uneven—at times boring, sometimes action-packed, occasionally disturbing and squirm-inducing—but, ultimately, the movie evokes a feeling that I like to get from my horror movies: sadness. You really have to stick with it, even when it gets weird, but it's worth it in the end. The movie is about a meteorologist in the early twentieth century who arrives on a small island to relieve the scientist who was there before him, only the scientist has gone missing and the rather taciturn lighthouse keeper—the only other person on the island—offers little by way of explanation. *Cold Skin* lives in the same place as Guillermo del Toro's *The Shape of Water* (2017) and Vincenzo Natali's *Splice (2009)*, by introducing the concept of a man-and-monster love story that can be uncomfortable to watch. Hey, that reminds me of something else that's long made straight, cisgendered people uncomfortable when they watch it. . . .

Crawl (Alexandre Aja, 2019)

Hey now! This was a fun movie. I mean, go into it with the appropriate expectations—it's a movie about some people stuck in the crawlspace of a house that's filled with bloodthirsty alligators during a Category 5 hurricane—but it's exciting, loud, and action-packed, and let's face it, alligators are *fucking scary.* They're dinosaurs, and they have no business still being in this world and still doing fucked up stuff like stealing peoples' pets and stuff. This movie delivers on all of its promises, though frankly, they could have trimmed the fat and taken out some of the drippy conversations between daddy and daughter. Yes, I wrote the word "daddy," and I did so mockingly. But it's a lotta fun and totally worth a watch!

Mega Shark vs. Giant Octopus (Jack Perez, 2009), *Mega Python vs. Gatoroid* (Mary Lambert, 2011), *Mega Shark vs. Mecha Shark* (Emile Edwin Smith, 2014)

Yeah, I know, I've gone off the deep end here. But hear me out. Debbie Gibson is in all of these movies, and she LOVES that she's in all of these movies. And if you can't appreciate Debbie Gibson being in horrible, B-grade horror movies because she really, truly likes them, then you're lacking a sense of kitsch that you really should refine, because you're missing out on some truly stupid-but-fun entertainment!

Sea Fever (Neasa Hardiman, 2019)

Sea Fever is a quiet Irish horror movie about a solemn marine biologist joining a fishing boat that becomes waylaid by a burgeoning deep-sea monster. A slow-paced, beautiful examination of the dangers we find in nature, how complex our relationship to them can be, and the responsibility we have to protect not only ourselves, but those very dangers as well. I found the acting to be up to snuff, the characters generally likable, and the sea creature great to look at. Also sort of an apt movie for the pandemic crisis of 2020 and beyond.

THE CALLS ARE COMING FROM INSIDE THE HOUSE

The Ways We Embody Horror Ourselves

My Mind Is a Basement Full of VHS Tapes

JOE

I started going to talk therapy in 2020. It was something I'd thought about doing for a long time but had been scared away by a bad therapist in my early twenties who hyperfocused on the "winter blues" and seemed uninterested in talking about the ways in which I felt I was harming myself. I'm glad I returned to therapy because it was the vehicle through which I was able to truly connect to and accept my queer identity, as detailed more fully in my introduction essay, "Hi Everyone, It's Me, Barbra."

Perhaps the most useful analogy for self-reflection I made during this time was an idea I hatched while talking to my therapist. I imagine that the inside of my brain is like a basement full of old boxes, each crammed full of VHS tapes, some labeled and some blank, in a carpeted room with wood panel walls. There's a scratchy plaid sofa from 1978 and a rabbit-ear television set with a heavy, metal VCR in the entertainment unit below. Sometimes when I'm trying to remember something, I feel like I'm popping a cassette into the VCR, pressing play, and watching an amalgamated memory. I don't know what the real term for this is, but a lot of my memories feel like they're a jumble of similar memories stuffed together into one scene that, more than anything, exemplifies the *feeling* of the memory rather than being one real, concrete memory. Most of the labeled VHS tapes are horror movies: bad memories. You know, the ones that get stuck in the VCR. I assume that lots of the unlabeled video cassettes are good memories, but who has the time to ruminate over those?

The feeling of watching one of these tapes is not dissimilar to watching a scary movie that I've seen before. When the memory begins to "play," I know what's going to happen. My heart beats faster. My head begins to swim with fear; I sometimes feel like shouting, "Don't you know he's right behind you!" or, "Don't open that door!" but I know that my shouting won't help to derail the plot of my memory any more than it could any other movie. The hiss of the tape doesn't care about my feelings, regardless of what's being shown, and adjusting the tracking only makes the memory more vivid, makes me dig into it deeper.

Only, sometimes I have to remind myself: these aren't horror movies. These aren't unchangeable pieces of art, created and directed and acted in by different people. These are my own memories. And while it's true that I still can't change them, I *can* change my response to them. I can alter how they make me *feel*, alter how devastated I feel when I rewatch them. Imagine that, a horror movie in which *I* am the actual heroine, and the ending might be written in stone, but I get to write the sequel.

And guess what? In this movie, the final girl lives. She exacts her revenge by choosing to pull that tape out of the VCR, put it back in its box with the other scary movies, and tape that box up. I've watched those movies, and I understand their plotlines—and you know what? I've learned a thing or two from them. I think it's time to start unboxing those tapes with the good memories to see what they have in store for me.

Not Pretty in Pink

GINA

During the summer of 1986, I was between my freshman and sophomore years of high school. Like most people that age, I was trying things on, figuring myself out identity-wise. I wasn't out of the closet yet, nowhere near—it'd be another ten years before I even realized I'm a lesbian—but I definitely wasn't connecting to the models of femininity around me. In my blue-collar hometown in the south suburbs of Chicago, I'm sure there were some women I'd have been keen to pattern on, but they weren't in my orbit.

The movies weren't helping either. The year 1986 brought us such classics as *Pretty in Pink, Ferris Bueller's Day Off, Crocodile Dundee,* and *Top Gun*—okay sure, if you say so, all great movies, but their female leads leave lots to be desired in terms of variety. I did get a hardcore ray of hope from *Jumping Jack Flash* featuring the cool, capable, and soooo not stereotypically feminine Terry Dolittle, played by Whoopi Goldberg, but the movie gave away a lot of what I loved about her when they hooked her up with a male British spy at the eleventh and a half hour. What was I looking for? I didn't know, or even really know I was looking for anything, but I was finding very few female characters I much liked, or who seemed much like me. They were all just . . . too girly. Of course, this was all complicated by an incident on the school bus in which two mean boys started calling me Gino Brandolino. Though I was always a bit of a tomboy, I intuitively veered away from looking too masculine: I definitely wanted to stay off the radar of serial bullies.

But then *Aliens* was released. There are several great female characters in it—Corporal Dietrich and Corporal Ferro (the pilot!), plus the incandescent Private Vasquez who was *BADASS*, *explicitly* masculine, and *explicitly* a lesbian. You'd think I'd have been happier to see Vasquez, but she was too much for me then. It was Ripley who caught my attention. I hadn't seen *Alien*, but flashbacks make it obvious that some terrible things happened to her involving, well, *an alien*. Nobody in the movie really cares about that, and worse, nobody really believes her: the truly harrowing story she has to tell is dismissed and she herself is discarded, left to find her own way after her trauma. She gets a very cute short (but not too short!) haircut, a standard-issue space jumpsuit, and a pair of Reebok hi-tops I deeply envied and makes do in a small apartment on a space station with Jonesy, the cat who lived through it all with her. She had my attention. To borrow a formulation *Seinfeld* used once: I didn't want to *date* Ripley; I wanted to *be* Ripley.

That didn't change as the plot developed: the colony on the planet where Ripley had her run-in with the alien goes silent, and people are worried. But not too worried, because surely it's not *aliens;* oh, okay maybe it is, but surely *they're not as bad* as Ripley made them out to be. But hey, better safe than sorry: the powers that be convince Ripley, acting as a sort of consultant, to accompany a unit of Marines to the colony to see what's going on. Then, long story short—and spoiler alert!—things go totally off the rails, most of the Marines are killed by (you guessed it) *aliens*, and Ripley is left to fight them pretty much single handedly. *And she does*, saving herself and the very few other survivors. *She* does that, by herself. To give due credit: an android who has been ripped in half by an alien gives some clutch help at the end, but really, that's the extent of it. This is Ripley's show.

The movie takes pains to telegraph that Ripley is straight: she has a very underdeveloped romantic thing with one of the male Marines, Corporal Hicks; and she has maternal feelings towards one of the surviving colonists, a little girl called Newt (motherhood isn't and never has been reserved for straight people alone, but in 1986, maternal instinct didn't really say "queer"). But this wasn't really an issue for me at age fourteen. What I liked is that Ripley was *Ripley* and that she *stayed* Ripley, right up to the end. I felt relief at the end of the movie not just because Ripley prevailed but also because she existed, even just as a fictional character. She gave me a way to be.

And I didn't even know I had *Alien*^{3} (1992) and *Alien Resurrection* (1997) to look forward to! In the former, Ripley has a shaved head, and in the latter, she has a modified body—one could very fairly argue that she becomes more and more queer. By the time *Alien Resurrection* came out, so had I, and I feel very much like Ripley accompanied me on that journey.

Horror has always been more willing than other genres to break the rules, to go places other movies won't. That's part of how it kindles fear in us. But violating expectations does more than just amp up the scares; it also makes the genre a crucible for social change—and, relatedly, moments of personal recognition and transformation. So it figures that it took a horror movie to deliver what I didn't even know I was looking for: a model for how to be female in our culture without being pretty in pink.

A Legacy of Homemade Costumes

JOE

In September of 2020—the deep lockdown era of the pandemic—I decided to go all out for Halloween. My local Victorian cemetery / favorite hangout, Laurel Hill Cemetery, was hosting their annual Rest In Peace 5k run, for which participants are encouraged to run in costume—only this time, it was virtual. The deal was, you were to get to the cemetery (or anywhere, really) and run or walk the 5k on your own. Once you'd done so, you could send in photos of your Halloween costume, and they'd pick a costume contest winner. It was just a bit of fun, a way to feel connected to them when everyone was stuck at home. They weren't checking to see if you'd really done the run. My partner Katie & I went for a long walk, then we decided to enter the contest and take it seriously.

Katie & I sometimes like to dress up but more often for events other than Halloween: I put together a pretty good Bender and she a convincing Claire for a thirtieth-anniversary showing of *The Breakfast Club* at a local movie theater. We even won a costume contest once at a goth synthpop party that was centered around another John Hughes film: I dressed like Duckie and K went as Iona for a *Pretty in Pink*-themed adult prom. (And we've got the Prom King and Prom Queen sashes to prove it.) This Halloween, though, we'd set our sights on something a little less *John Hughes* and a little more . . . *dramatic*: Joan & Tina.

Up until the point I'd watched it for the first time, I thought *Mommie Dearest* was a horror movie. I could picture the white face, the wire hanger, the overwrought, sometimes-clownish makeup and acting. The shouting, the disharmony. Early in our relationship, K finally sat me down to watch it, and I was hooked. Just like two other movies she introduced me to, *Grey Gardens* and *Sunset Boulevard*, *Mommie Dearest* is actually pretty psychologically scary, but the cartoonish dramatics try to hide that from you until the fourth, fifth, twelfth time you watch it.

K looks a little like Tina: the fair skin, the blond hair, the cute little face that scrunches up when she's worried. I don't happen to look anything like Joan Crawford (or, to make the correct distinction, Faye Dunaway as Joan Crawford. Put down your pitchforks, fellas, I know that's not *really* Joan.) But I'm not afraid to try my hand at a new costume. I spent an afternoon searching online and found a pattern for a no-sew tulle skirt then spent a few evenings knotting tulle before searching Etsy for a brown-and-gold sequined top large enough to fit my big man-shoulders. After that, we searched for and found a suitable wig that Katie helped me style. We were recreating the famous garden scene, you know, when Joan cuts down the rose bushes: *Tina, bring me the ax!* We even made cardboard axes and garden shears. We won the costume contest, which we'd allowed ourselves to dream was possible, since our look was that good.

One thing I wasn't counting on: when I was all dressed up as Joan, I looked in the mirror and thought of my mom. My mom doesn't look anything like Joan Crawford, and I don't especially look like my mom, even when wearing a wig, sequined top, and homemade tulle skirt. But when I was twenty-two, my mom taught me how to sew. She got out her old machine, plugged it in at the dining room table, showed me how to thread the needle, then pulled it all apart and had me thread it a few times for practice. I had the idea to create felt pouches that I could adorn with patches, pipe cleaners, and other crafty knick-knacks to hold the six issues of my first-ever zine, *Today Terrific*. Once I caught the sewing bug, a new world opened up to me. First, I made a hoodie for myself (which I then put through the wash and it shrunk so much I couldn't ever use it again). Next, a blue hoodie with bumblebee lining—this time I washed the fabric first! I added a hood and pockets to a big, heavy wool cardigan, purses that I sold on Etsy, a ukulele backpack out of an old T-shirt. I even made a messenger bag out of fabric from an old couch that I used for a decade.

I don't think I could have made that Joan costume without my mother, not only for encouraging me to make my own clothing but for a lifetime of costumes she made for me herself. Deep in her photobooks are pictures of me, age three, wearing a felt M&M costume that she made me for Halloween. She was particularly proud of a Link costume from *Legend of Zelda*, consisting of a felt tunic and hat with an aluminum foil and cardboard shield. I had a full felt Santa outfit, complete with cotton-ball beard; warlock cloaks; magician top hats. Whatever I wanted to be, with a seeming wave of her magic wand (and a few hours at the sewing machine), she could make it. I feel so proud to have carried that on and proud of my mom for not discouraging me from learning to sew, even if it was hard for some people in my life to see me do something that was, in their eyes, less than masculine.

This is the heart of the horror behind movies like *Mommie Dearest* and *Grey Gardens*: the psychological horror of the heteronormative family pushing its agenda from all (or at least most) sides. And I wasn't even out when I was little! But the bullies are always the first to know, right? The amount of gay-bashing and sniping that I endured, almost entirely from extended family members, was intense even then. The horror of poorly set boundaries, acceptance of abuse so *we can just have a nice time.* The horror of: *just tune out what he says, he doesn't really mean it,* of: *don't let our perfect Christmas get spoiled because you can't laugh off a little joke.* Yeah, a "little joke" that's actually a wrenching indignity or slur masked with a smile.

The most wonderful aspect of horror movies is that the monster is almost always an allegory: sure, there are some movies in which the monster is just a monster, but often, the monster is a lot more than that. Sometimes the monster is a feeling you get when you're alone, a niggling doubt you can't get rid of, a swipe you take at yourself and you don't know why. Sometimes, the monster is the voice of your uncle, your cousin, your sibling. The manifestation of a comment your father made when he was drinking.

Sometimes the monster is the Joan Crawford of *Mommie Dearest,* a clownish entertainer who you love to hate, who terrorized her own helpless children. It's only until the third watching of this overwrought and dramatized movie of her life that she starts to seem too vitriolic to be funny.

Getting to Be the Victim

GINA

When my sister and I got my mom to rent *Halloween III* from the video store for us in the mid-1980s, we didn't know what we were in for. We'd seen *Halloween* and *Halloween II*, so we expected more Michael Myers because, *duh*, it's *Halloween.*

But *Halloween III* is actually a departure from Michael Myers that tells a totally different story (though, in a very cool and very meta move, it uses references to the original *Halloween*, and even shows it playing on TV). I'm going to try hard not to include any major spoilers because I beg you to *please* experience this under-appreciated gem for yourself—on Halloween night, if you can. But, in a nutshell, *Halloween III* is about a nefarious plot that hinges on mass-produced Halloween masks for children. The story is set in the week leading up to Halloween, and the main protagonist is Dan Challis, a medical doctor with a bit of a drinking problem. He has an intrepid medical examiner as a sidekick, and before they manage to discover and confront the main villain, they have to contend with a whole passel of affectless, lurking men in understated business suits. If that makes the bad guys of the movie sound corporate, yeah, they kind of are, but also they kind of aren't. They're into human sacrifice; they've stolen one of Stonehenge's giant stones; and they do some science-y magic, or magic-y science. Overall, there's a definite "mad scientist" vibe to the movie, but "mad scientist" circa 1982, which is when the movie was released. A gloomy, dark factory stands in for a laboratory, and efficient-looking men rush around in white lab coats (with understated business suits underneath, probably), constantly adjusting panels of electrical equipment with a million dials and switches.

And speaking of 1982, *Halloween III* is by no definition timeless; one of its greatest charms is how thoroughly of its era it is. Watching this movie now gives me such nostalgia for the 1980s in general, and in particular for early 1980s technology, so ungainly and so much more entangled with its human users. Characters listen to the radio at work, in the car, lying in bed, reaching to fumble with the tuning knob when they want to change channels. Televisions (then as now) are ubiquitous, but in the 1980s they were so much more massive—so much more *a thing.* At one point a character kicks in the screen of a TV and exposes a deep hole, the inside of the TV tube; it's like looking into the guts of an animal. And phones! Old-school phones are all over the place. At several critical points, Challis has to find a pay phone and frantically digs into his pockets for change. Near the end of the movie, he runs breathless up to a service station yelling, "Your phone! Your phone! Where is it? *It's life and death!"* The existence of cell phones has by and large robbed us of the dread that comes with characters desperately searching for a public phone in movies, but it's palpable in *Halloween III.* Not to mention the private phones in the movie, with their curly cords hugging the wrists of the characters using them. Most of the movie's phones are touch tone, but there's at least one rotary phone, its satisfying *clickclickclickclick sliiiiiiiiiiiiide* noise so familiar and even comforting to me now. But the technology that takes the 1980s cake, you see in the opening credits: while foreboding synth music plays, a pixelated ultra-orange jack-o'-lantern gets slowly, painstakingly constructed on a computer screen. If you imagine that, back in the day, Atari had a pumpkin-carving video game, you're on the right track.

Okay, okay: so I love the walk down tech memory lane this movie gives me now. But why'd I love it so much back then, when my mom rented it for my sister and me? It had to be around 1984; I'd have been twelve, my sister seven. We were expecting another movie in which teenagers were in peril. What we got is a movie in which *kids* are the main endangered characters—kids like my sister and me waiting impatiently for the day they got to go trick-or-treating and excitedly trying on their Halloween masks all the time. The masks, remember, are the heart of the nefarious plot in *Halloween III*. I hadn't seen very many films—certainly no *adult* films like this one—in which kids were at the heart of a nefarious plot.

But for a kid of twelve, I was pretty well-versed in nefarious plots: As I mention in my essay "Summer of Dread," I grew up in the Chicago suburbs, where in 1982 several people died when someone put cyanide in Tylenol capsules before they left store shelves. I lived mere miles away from the federal penitentiary Stateville, where serial killers John Wayne Gacy and Richard Speck were jailed—and like all local kids, I knew their stories. In 1983, I watched the made-for-TV movie *Adam*; in 1984, I watched *Fatal Vision*. I knew from nefarious plots.

And the plot in *Halloween III* focused on kids! Kids like me! At the end, when the plot comes to a head, we get shown kids trick-or-treating in various cities all across the U.S.—I remember thinking, *one of them is probably gonna be my city*! The main villain even says at one point, in answer to Challis asking him why he's carrying out his awful plot, "I do love a good joke, and this is the best. It's even a joke on the children." I *loved* that kids like me were so heavily implicated in the story; it was a rare treat. America in the 1980s wasn't really oriented to kids; there weren't play dates, a ton of after-school activities, or even after-care. I myself was a latch-key kid; both my parents worked; the TV kept me occupied. I watched so many reruns that to this day I can recite Carol Burnett sketches and *Laverne and Shirley* scenes to you; I can sing you the entire theme song to *Good Times.* It wasn't a hardship and I'm not complaining; actually, I think people who grew up in the 1980s have an increasingly rare kind of resilience precisely *because* the adult world didn't really accommodate us.

So to have a movie that made *kids* the focus, that put *us* in peril? Strange as it is to say, for me, it was an honor to be able to so closely identify with the endangered characters. Sure, I'd identified with Laurie Strode from the original *Halloween* but only by imagining I was older. This was how all horror movies worked for me back then, compelling me to envision myself as a grown-up or as being closer than I was to being a grown-up, facing danger. But for *Halloween III,* I didn't have to imagine my way into the shoes of the characters facing the danger; they were pretty much exactly like my shoes, or at the very least the right size! It made me feel important in a way I hadn't before. For a change, characters like me weren't on the sidelines, tucked into bed upstairs, or safe at a neighbor's house. They were in the thick of things.

Listening for Ghosts

GINA

"The story had held us, round the fire, sufficiently breathless," the first line read, and I was riveted. I was twenty years old and reading Henry James's 1898 novella, *The Turn of the Screw*, for the first time. I loved it immediately. That first line gripped me, drawing me into the group gathered by the fire. This opening to James's novella is part of a frame story describing that group of friends celebrating Christmas together in an old English manor, trading ghost stories, as was the Victorian holiday tradition. The story that the frame story opens onto—the main story of the novella—is told by Douglas, one of the friends gathered for the holiday celebration. But it isn't Douglas's story. He reads it from a handwritten account recorded by the governess who lived through it. And that story, the governess's story that Douglas tells, isn't the story described in the arresting first line. A *different* story has the gathered group in its thrall when the novella opens, and it's a story we never get to hear.

We do get some glimpses into that untold story. One of the listeners remarks that it was "the only case he had met in which such a visitation had fallen on a child." And our unnamed narrator fills in a few particulars:

> The case, I may mention, was that of an apparition in just such an old house as had gathered us for the occasion—and appearance, of a dreadful kind, to a little boy sleeping in the room with his mother and waking her up in the terror of it; waking her not to dissipate his dread and soothe him to sleep again, but to encounter also herself, before she had succeeded in doing so, the same sight that had shocked him.

But that's all we learn of that story. Soon after these scant details are shared, Douglas says: well, if you liked that story, I have an even better one, and then tells the governess's story. And it's a *humdinger* of a story; I've re-read it many, many times. It remains one of my top three favorite ghost stories, and to be honest, top three favorite stories of any kind. But as captivating as the governess's story is, I always leave *The Turn of the Screw* a little unsatisfied, wondering about that other story that we readers don't get to hear, the one that has the friends gathered around the fire reeling at the beginning. I have a lot of questions about that story: How old was the little boy? What were the events leading up to the visitation; why did it show up? Who was the ghost? What did it want? Why did it appear to this boy and his mother? What made it scary to them? The mother, we are told, does get the boy back to sleep in the story, so the ghost must have gone, but how did they get it to leave, or did it leave of its own accord? I've never been able to let go of that shadowy story; it lives in me with the same intensity as the governess's tale—maybe more intensity, as I cling more tightly to the paucity of details it offers me. I wish I could hear *that* story.

Since my first reading of *The Turn of the Screw*, I've become a pretty industrious reader of ghost stories. I've noticed in other ghost stories the shadows of stories like that one at the start of *The Turn of the Screw*—stories mentioned in passing in the main narrative, alluded to but not shared. Earlier, I used the word *untold* to describe the story we don't get to hear in *The Turn of the Screw,* but that's not really an accurate way to characterize that story or these others like it that I've noticed. These stories aren't exactly *un*told; there's always the sense that *someone* gets to hear them, just not us. Writers definitely make a choice to include them, or to include reference to them, at least, but then they make other choices that make the barely-there stories sort of evanesce. I wouldn't say this kind of shadowy story is a convention of the genre—it doesn't occur that regularly—but I've noticed it enough times that I started keeping track of occurrences of it. I have too many to share the whole list, but here are a few examples: W.W. Jacobs, who you might know because he wrote the famous story "The Monkey's Paw," has a ghost story called "Jerry Bundler" with an untold story right at the start, like the one in *The Turn of the Screw*:

> Three ghost stories, never known to fail before, had fallen flat; there was too much noise outside, too much light within. The fourth story was told by an old hand with more success; the streets were quiet, and he had turned the gas out.
>
> In the flickering light of the fire, as it shone on the glasses and danced with shadows on the walls, the story proved so enthralling that George, the waiter, whose presence had been forgotten, created a very disagreeable sensation by suddenly starting up from a dark corner and gliding silently from the room.
>
> "That's what I call a good story," said one of the men, sipping his hot whisky.

And that's all we hear of that story. No hot whisky for us, and no story. Edith Wharton has a similar start in her story "The Eyes":

> We had been put in the mood for ghosts, that evening, after an excellent dinner at our old friend Culwin's, by

> a tale of Fred Murchard's—the narrative of a strange personal visitation.
>
> Seen through the haze of our cigars, and by the drowsy gleam of a coal fire, Culwin's library, with its oak walls and dark old bindings, made a good setting for such evocations; and ghostly experiences at first hand being, after Murchard's opening, the only kind acceptable to us, we proceeded to take stock of our group and tax each member for a contribution.

We do get to hear *a* story, but not ol' Fred's story. Lest you think, based on those examples, *Oh, this is just a cool way to start a ghost story*: The untold story doesn't always come at the beginning. Here's one from near the end of Sheridan Le Fanu's story "An Account of Some Strange Disturbances in Aungier Street":

> "And what did they say of Nicholas Spaight?" I asked.
>
> "Oh, for that matter, it's soon told," she answered.
>
> And she certainly did relate a very strange story, which so piqued my curiosity, that I took occasion to visit the ancient lady, her mother, from whom I learned many curious particulars. Indeed, I am tempted to tell the tale, but my fingers are weary, and I must defer it.

Damn those weary fingers! Denied again!

These are less stories than *ghosts of stories:* difficult to see, often unacknowledged. Though we don't get to hear them so don't always know for sure, they usually seem to be *about* ghosts, but that isn't what makes them ghosts of stories; it's their own in-between narrative existence that does. They seem designed to be elusive, to slip by us barely noticed or unnoticed, and I think most people do read right past them. I'm curious about *all* these ghosts of stories; I want to hear them all. In my heart of hearts, I think I'd trade all the told stories that they exist in the shadows of to be able to hear them—even that main story in *The Turn of the Screw*, the governess's story, honestly.

I've spent a lot of time wondering about these ghosts of stories. I feel an anxious insistence that they be real stories; I can't, won't believe that they're just narrative blanks, facades the writers use like scenery to propel the main story. I think these stories surely must exist in the minds of writers who include them in passing, but they decline to narrate them for their own reasons. What *are* those reasons, though? I know that similar barely told stories must exist in the stories of other genres, but I genuinely doubt that they're as regular a feature in them as they are in ghost stories: *Ghost stories* seem to breed *ghosts of stories.* My ability to pretty easily compile a list of ghost stories in which ghosts of stories occur suggests that they're no, not a convention, but at least a sort of tic or habit of the ghost story genre specifically. I've long wanted to be able to explain these ghosts of stories as a phenomenon specific to ghost stories, but I haven't had much success with that. And really, I just want to hear them.

And that gave me an idea. Maybe the key to my finally having a handle on these ghosts of stories isn't the genre. Maybe the key is the reader, *this* reader. I think my interest, well nigh obsession, with these stories marks me as a lesbian of a certain age—an age that makes me old enough to remember a time when books like the one you're reading now didn't exist, when stories about queers were a lot harder to come by. Most times, you only really heard those stories if you knew how to listen. I remember a time before I came out, before I even knew I was a lesbian, when an adult woman I knew must have recognized my queerness because she was queer herself, though not openly at the time. *The Silence of the Lambs* had just premiered, and the woman had seen it and loved it. She was talking to me about about Jodie Foster (lolsob who was then herself a closeted lesbian, *OMG will someone in this essay please come out already?*), making fluttery hand gestures around her heart while she enthused about what a smart and cool character Clarice Starling is. I was eighteen years old and very naïve at the time, and I didn't get it. Later, I got it. I was sorry I missed it at the time, especially when I eventually told similar stories of my own to people I recognized as queer and understood the stakes of doing so.

I picked the story above almost at random—to be honest, ultimately I picked it because, being about *Silence of the Lambs,* it was horror-themed—but I have many other similar stories involving my mailman, my realtor, an elderly lady I used to run errands for, and so on. Such stories used to be a regular way for queer people to communicate information about themselves. Thankfully, this is increasingly less the case; the days of having to hide what used to be referred to as "the love that dare not speak its name" are mostly in the past. But find any queer person over the age of forty-five—if they're from a small town, thirty-five—and they'll be able to tell you stories like my Jodie Foster one. There was always a main story, one everyone heard ("Man, Jodie Foster plays a *great* character!") and another story ( ) told so indirectly most people didn't even notice it was a story at all. Only those who knew what they were listening for would get it. And you'd *get it,* though you wouldn't have every detail spelled out for you or have all your questions answered. It's hard to explain what a gift hearing such a story was. It meant someone trusted you enough to ask you to bear witness to them, to *see* them in a way they had little, or maybe no, other audience for. On the other hand, telling such a story was like being a ghost wanting desperately to be seen—and then someone seeing you, being willing to see you. And bonus if they weren't freaked out.

I'm not saying that all those ghosts of stories I've kept a list of are about queer people. Though more than a few people have explained the experience of being queer using the figure of the ghost, including me just now in that last paragraph and elsewhere in this book in my essay "Lesbian Ghost," I don't think there's a queer person tucked into every ghost story, even the untold ones. The kinship I'm pointing out isn't about *content*; it's about *style*. Like I said earlier, the ghosts of stories aren't exactly *untold* stories; they're told just enough to indicate a presence—the presence of another story—if you're paying enough attention or the right kind of attention to register it. Queer stories like my Jodie Foster example work the same way. And as in the Jodie Foster example, *getting* the story shifts something and *not getting it* deprives you of something. For queer stories, the payoff was camaraderie, a sense of belonging—plus, you were acknowledging the identity of the person brave enough to tell the story. You were saying to them, *I see you.* What hangs in the balance with the ghosts of stories is very similar. Seeing the ghost of a story more intensely embeds you in the narrative; you become one of the friends gathered around the fire in *The Turn of the Screw*, one of the listeners sipping hot whisky and being startled by George the waiter in "Jerry Bundler." You get to be one of the cigar smokers hanging on Fred Murchard's tale in "The Eyes" and tag along with the narrator of "An Account of Some Strange Disturbances in Aungier Street" to hear the ancient lady's tale. In a sense, you can claim camaraderie with the listeners in the story; you have earned a spot in their ranks. Even more, being drawn into the story in these ways implicates you in the narrative process by goading you into imagining the whole shape of the ghost of a story from the bits and pieces you're given. And that act of imagination gives you another ghost for your trouble—the ghost from the ghost of a story in addition to the one in the ghost story itself. You earn the right to say to that ghost, who most readers miss entirely: *I see you.*

Sliving for the Dead

JOE

It'd be hard for me to summarize the sheer number of hours I've spent watching paranormal television. Ghost hunters, experts reviewing amateur footage, YouTube ghost sighting compilations, you name it. I literally called my partner Katie when the newest season of *Paranormal Caught on Camera* was released and was like, *Hey, we're not doing anything tonight, right?* Also, I grew up in the nineties in New Jersey, so you know I had my *Weird NJ* subscription, a magazine that collected dozens of eyewitness stories of hauntings, ghastly tales, and just good ol' fashioned kooks-being-kooks. All in all I've spent a lot of time thinking about ghosts. I also spent many years of my not-yet-out life wondering why I cried so, so much during every queer show and movie I watched, including many seasons of *RuPaul's Drag Race*. Seriously, it's like a game, you could bet that I couldn't get through a single episode without crying, and you'd win that bet every. single. time. I guess my body knew something about me before my mind was ready. So when I heard about *Living for the Dead*, a queer reality ghost hunting show from the creators of *Queer Eye* and executive producer Kristen Stewart, I felt like it was made specifically for the audience of me.

In *Living for the Dead*, we follow our ghoul gang of five queer ghosties, each with their own specialty—Juju, the witch; Alex, the ghost hunter; Ken, the tarot reader; Logan, the medium; and Roz, the researcher—each with their own strong personality that exudes inclusivity, comfort, warmth, and humor. No complaints from me on the casting. Each member of the team is endearing and intelligent (though I do have my favorite: I'd share a donut with Roz any day!), and their chemistry is strong from the beginning. They're all well-suited to taking care of their clients with tenderness and a dash of wry humor, be they the owners of a haunted clown motel, the staff at a haunted theater, or the owner of a funeral home-turned-headquarters-turned . . . well, that chapter of the building's life has not yet begun.

Each episode approaches its particular haunting as a problem to be solved in order to help their client heal from some trauma or reach betterment in another way, a la *Queer Eye*. You know, a young man needs to shake a possibly demonic attachment before proposing to his girlfriend, or the girls working at a nightclub want to feel safer in their environment. It's a common narrative in queer media, because it's a common experience for queer people: accepting and processing trauma instead of ignoring it and soldiering on. *Living for the Dead* really shines when it shifts its focus from the undead to the, well, more alive. The cast and their clients share tender moments as well as stories of intolerance and acceptance. These conversations lead to *We're Here*-like moments, to invoke the name of another excellent gay reality show, the one where a group of drag queens go into different cities to meet someone who needs help in an effort to spread acceptance and love. These tender conversations speak to the "exqueerience" of coming out, finding safety in community when you didn't have it in childhood, and promoting kindness towards others, regardless of how they live their lives. They're really special moments.

But while *Living for the Dead* is wrapped in such a charming shell, its actual spirit work left me a little cold-to-the-touch, my battery a little drained. The show is missing the organic nature that's so strong in most successful ghost hunting shows. TAPS, the organization behind the first major ghost hunting show, *Ghost Hunters,* existed for almost ten years before the show aired, and you really felt it in the way the investigators related to each other. They had two strong leaders in Jason Hawes and Grant Wilson, and each member of the crew knew their job. *Paranormal State* followed a group of students who ran a ghost hunting organization at their university. *Ghost Adventures* had a team that was assembled for the show, but had clear leadership in Zak Bagans. Ghost hunting shows seem to work best when there is a personality who is, more or less, in charge—someone to focus the mission. My major issue with *Living for the Dead* is that the goal of each episode feels scattershot. Instead of following a team with one goal—today, we're going into this prison with a spirit box to communicate with the spirits—*Living for the Dead* at times feels like everyone is in their own room, practicing their own craft while the others look on, waiting for their own time to use their particular gift. That time was usually given, which left a frighteningly small amount of time for the actual issue at hand. However, each episode ended positively, and the clients always felt better, even if it was a little hard to trace what *actually happened* in each episode to change the attitude of the client besides, well, having a group of warm, friendly people actually listening to and uplifting them.

Which is one of the core tenets of reality TV, you know? This is where *Living for the Dead* truly shines and separates itself from its more hetero-focusing counterparts. Particularly in life-improvement shows, a category that ghost hunting shows often fall under: sure, sometimes an episode is just a bunch of doofuses running around an abandoned mental hospital scaring themselves, but often they're in someone's real house, a person who's upset and scared and needs help. Sometimes that help comes from an exorcism by a local exorcist. Sometimes that help comes in the form of a group of people coming in and saying, *Hey, we believe you, and you're not alone.* Either way, shows like this can exist to let people know they aren't alone with their problems, that they can find someone to be on their side. And that's a really great thing.

It makes me think about one of the things I've always hated about ghost hunting shows: So many of them focus on a tough guy who often resorts to antagonizing and provoking the dead to get a response in an effort to prove that ghosts exist. Guess what, fellas? It's not working. I can't help but feel these dudes are being so incredibly disrespectful to what, at least they think, is the spirit of a deceased person. Why so aggro?

I have to smile when I think about this being the *queer* ghost hunting show: since coming out, I've been met with acceptance, joy, and inclusion from the queer community, something that can feel hard to come by in predominantly straight spaces, even those largely bound by a similar interest or around a community event. It's not hard to believe this is the show where each member of the cast takes their time to carefully and thoughtfully communicate with the dead. That on its own is meaningful: kindness, to the living *and the dead*, is a real mark of something right in the world.

Lost Girls

GINA

Twice in my life, I've been derailed by horror.

Not shaken up in the usual way, the way we fans of the genre *love*—like making us squint into the mirror to be sure Candyman isn't there in the background, peer into the corners of dark rooms to make sure Charlie from *Hereditary* isn't in the shadows, wonder if every person behind us on the sidewalk is the monster from *It Follows,* and so on. Lingering effects like these are totally expected and, for me anyway, they're part of the joy of horror. It makes the ordinary world a little more interesting and exciting. But this isn't what I mean.

Twice in my life, I was *derailed* by horror. Think of a train, going along smoothly, suddenly brought up short, thrown off its tracks, wheels spinning in the air. That's what I mean. Twice, horror wrecked me.

Here was the first time: One late summer afternoon in 1983 I was lazily flipping through TV channels and came across *The Exorcist.* Let's not spend too much time thinking about who made the dubious decision to put *The Exorcist* on network TV (Network! It wasn't even cable!) of a summer afternoon. I was eleven years old and transfixed. The scene I happened to tune into was Regan's exorcism. She was a girl not much more than my age, wearing a nightgown like ones I had. But hers was covered in vomit, and her face ravaged with cuts and sores. I watched in horror as she said terrible and alarming things in the devil's voice to the two priests trying to help her and ultimately levitated above the bed while they looked on in fearful amazement, chanting the rite. I didn't watch more than that single scene—I think my mom walked by and was like, "What the hell are you watching?!" But it was more than enough.

The second time takes a little more setting up: It was again a late summer afternoon, this time in 2015, and I was driving around doing errands and listening to NPR (I was forty-three years old this time). Wes Craven had recently died, and Fresh Air was rerunning an old interview Terry Gross had done with him right after she'd seen Craven's *Last House on the Left.* Her approach to him in the interview was basically, *OMG WHAT IS THE MATTER WITH YOU, THAT YOU MADE THIS MOVIE?* She thought it was disgusting; she told him so. Essentially asked to explain himself, to give some accounting for what he was trying to do in the movie, Craven told this story from his childhood:

> We lived next to a railroad yard and . . . I got a mail-order bow and arrow set. I mean, you know, a legitimate one. And I started hunting. And the only thing to hunt there was rats because the railroad yard had this area where they kicked grain out of cattle cars. And there were a lot of rats. And I started—almost by accident—started hunting rats. And I went a whole year before I got near to even hitting a rat. It turned out they were extremely canny, very, very alert. And I never got close to one for the first six months because I wasn't that good a shot. But I kept practicing, I kept hunting these

> things and kept wishing I would get one. Finally one evening, almost dark, I took a shot at a rat after stalking it for half an hour, after sitting quietly and waiting for it to come out just right. I shot and I hit the thing. And at that moment, this little tiny animal let out this enormous scream that echoed over all the boxcars in the stockyard and chilled me to the bone. I realized that what I had been thinking and fantasizing was totally different from what I had actually done. And not only that, but the thing was still alive. And I went down and I said, well, it is a rat, you know? I—nobody likes rats, but I had to kill it. And it took a lot of killing to kill that rat and it continued screaming for a long time. I'll tell you, when I was done I was totally drained. I was totally shocked by what—not only what I had done for amusement, but how fiercely that thing struggled to stay alive. And that moment never left me. You know, I never again hunted, never killed. But I remembered how hard just a rat struggled to be alive.

That, Craven explained, is what he was going for in the movie: he wanted to show just how hard the living will struggle to be alive. We'd all become inured to stylized depictions of violence, he said, and he wanted to shake audiences up, make them really think about what they're seeing on the screen. Listening in my car, I thought: Huh! What a thoughtful guy, and what a smart thing to say about what horror can show us! I'd never seen *Last House on the Left*, so when I got home, first thing, I found a twenty-minute clip online so I could see what Craven was talking about. And I did.

I should have taken Terry Gross's reaction more to heart. I've never described the scene I watched to another person, and I'm not going to do it now; it's too graphic and disturbing. It involved the protagonists Mari and Phyllis in the clutches of Krug and his gang. They don't die in the scene; it'd have been better for them if they did, frankly. They were the rats, and they did struggle. I watched, riveted, to the end of the clip, and I haven't been the same since.

Now look, I'm no stranger to horror: I'm over fifty years old, and I've been steeped in horror stories for all of those years. I'm an English teacher, and among my course offerings include several different horror courses; rarely does a semester pass when I'm not teaching at least one. What I read for pleasure, what movies and TV shows I watch? Pretty much all horror.

And it's not like no other horror gets to me. The little girls in *The Shining*, when they show up stock still, holding hands, and chanting "Come play with us"—*gaaaaah!* The preacher Kane in *Poltergeist II*, when he comes calling in a preternatural thunderstorm and delivers a front-stoop sermon that ends with "You're gonna die in there, all of you!"—chilling! That girl from *The Ring* in any scene at all, literally pick any one—pee-my-pants terror! But these are the kind of scares I love, the kind I talked about earlier, that light up all horror fans. Maybe different scenes for different folks, but same feeling. Scary fun!

What those bits of *The Exorcist* and *Last House on the Left* did to me was different. It was deeper, more abiding, and not fun. There was no thrill; there was only dread that grew and grew. To my eyes, that was all there was to the scenes I watched. Darkness all the way down. I've spent a lot of time thinking about why these two scenes, witnessed at such different moments of my life so far, have affected me so strongly. I mean, they *are* pieces of horror; of course they're supposed to make me feel scared, but they've become parts of my psyche; they surface unbidden when I least expect them, when I'm freaked out, deeply shaken, or feel endangered. In short, they haunt me. I don't have any definitive answers about why they've gotten lodged inside me so deeply, but I have a theory.

In very different ways, these two scenes dramatize one of my deepest fears: losing yourself, by which I mean being alive in your body but not in control of it, somehow absent from it. One set of my grandparents owned a tavern and the other made very strong home-made Italian wine, so you can guess what I saw a lot of as a kid that planted the seeds of fear and anxiety about this condition. I'm not talking about drunk people who had a few drinks, or five. I'm talking about drunk people who were blotto. What scared me back then, when I was young, was that people I loved and knew well were transformed into unpredictable, mercurial, histrionic, sometimes violent strangers by drinking. I wasn't just scared *of* them, though, to be sure, there was some of that. I was scared *for* them: where'd they go? Were they still in there somewhere? How would they find their way back? As you can guess, these childhood experiences have left me not much of a drinker, and being around intensely drunk people now, seeing this loss of self in them, is just as scary to me now as it was when I was a kid.

I think Regan, Mari, and Phyllis tap into this old fear of mine, one that never left me, and put their own awful spins on it. Those scenes I watched tell the scariest story I know in different ways. Losing yourself to a sinister force in a bottle is one thing, but to a gang of demented killers? *To the devil?* They take that old fear and elaborate it in ways that filled me—that still fill me—with questions: When you lose yourself, do you know it's happening? Does something of you remain, stifled, small, and tortured deep inside you, testament to the loss? Is it worse if it does or doesn't? What of yourself could possibly be left to reclaim after such a violation? When it happens to a child, is it scarier for her? What happens when you're with your friend and it happens—to both of you? How quickly are you turned against each other? If your body is forced into performing unspeakable acts, what happens to your mind? What part of any of this is just plain human depravity; what part is supernatural? Can you tell the difference? Does it even matter?

See? *Derailed.*

I don't think either of these movies, watched in their entirety, would have led me down this wretched path. Watching a whole movie, you get context, more of the actual story and less of what's going on in your own head. And almost always, you get closure. I've seen *The Exorcist* all the way through lots of times now; I know Regan is (mostly) all right at the end. I don't think I'll ever see all of *Last House on the Left*, but I know what happens—no rescue, but at least vengeance, resolution. In my mind, though, Regan is always full of the devil floating over that bed, and Mari and Phyllis are always . . . well, I won't say; I can't. Suffice to say they're *there*, but gone. They're all three frozen in time like I saw them in those scenes, lost forever.

I have complicated feelings about the marks these two pieces of horror left on me. On the one hand, yes—*of course!*—these scenes still bother me. What bothers me worse, what actually harrows me, is remembering my feelings during my first encounters with them, that cold, dark dread settling in deeper and deeper. I don't want to see either scene ever again, but even more than that, I'm relieved that it isn't possible for me to experience seeing either one for the first time ever again. But on the other hand, perversely, these scenes make me feel safe. They signal to me that I've found some kind of edge to my own terror, a buoy that marks the deep end for me. I've been out that far. And I have to admire the power of the genre, to be able to show me that edge, to take me out that far. That's a lot for a story to give you, even if it comes with a price.

It Came from the Closet: Quick Horror Recs on the Theme of Personal Horror

It Came From the Closet: Queer Reflections on Horror (ed. Joey Vallese, Feminist Press, 2022)

It Came From the Closet is an anthology of essays by queer writers who are horror fans, each choosing to dissect one movie that's made a lasting impression on them. Written with warmth and heart, wit and erudition, it only took me about halfway through the first essay in the book to begin crying on my way to work on the train downtown. In a razor sharp and deeply poignant essay on *The Exorcist* called "A Demon Girl's Guide to Life," author S. Trimble gives us the ultimate guide to queer artists reflecting on how horror movies shape, define, and refine their identities. Well, second only to the horror essays I've read by one Gina Brandolino. . . .

The Evil Dead Franchise

Where most horror franchises specialize in trying to scare the bejeezus out of you, Evil Dead focuses on the fun you can have with horror. The series is also just great to talk about, as it's one of those things that brings people together—all horror fans seem to love *The Evil Dead* and series lead Bruce Campbell, myself included. Best of all, it launched Campbell's long and wonderful career.

The first entry in the series, 1981's *The Evil Dead*, is a serious and terrifying movie: a group of young'ns head to a cabin for a vacation getaway, only to find the cabin contains something of a beginner's guide to calling forth an ancient evil that will consume and torture everyone involved in its summoning before loosing itself on the general public. It *also* features some great early eighties everyday fashion and loads of unintentionally funny scenes. Its 1987 sequel, *The Evil Dead II*, is one of the strangest concepts I've seen actualized: a self-proclaimed "re-quel" that both remakes the original and continues the storyline, a way to sort of retool the series to be more comedy-oriented than straight horror. In this one, Bruce Campbell's protagonist Ash Williams comes to the cabin, this time with only his girlfriend for a romantic getaway, but they *still* manage to unleash an ancient evil. Somehow, the movie totally works, both standing alone and as a followup to the original, and it is just as enjoyable as the first, even if it largely trades in terror for demented comedy.

Then, 1992 saw the release of *Army of Darkness*, in which Ash is accidentally transported to the Middle Ages and must gain the trust of King Arthur in order to help vanquish the invading skeleton army of "Deadites" with his now-iconic chainsaw hand and a shotgun. Very silly, I know, but very fun to watch. Then, after a pretty-good-but-ultimately-forgettable reboot *Evil Dead* film in 2013, the series leaned back into fun in 2015 with *Ash vs. Evil Dead*, a three-season romp from Showtime that follows the canon of the storyline, featuring a much older Ash who now recruits some younger helpers to once again take on the Deadites as they invade our world. I groaned when I saw the announcement for the series, but it's really quite fun, and I always love to see Lucy Lawless. She's great: she's really progressive, a great ally to LGBTQ+ causes, a good actor, and seems like a really beautiful person all around!

Lastly, 2023's *Evil Dead Rise* is a disgusting good time. You may be surprised to learn this, but I, Joe, writer of horror movie zines, keeper of a Google Sheet with over five hundred horror movie reviews, am really squeamish about gross horror movie stuff. But I was able to shelve that distaste and enjoy *Evil Dead Rise* for its rollicking good horror sensibility. In a sentence, an alt mother to three weirdos in their funky-but-rundown artist apartment is possessed by the same demon from the earlier films, and she says and does some fucked up and funny shit until the demon is stopped. It's a little light on actual content and spends too much time with itself—seriously, it could have been a whole twenty minutes shorter—but it's pretty exciting. The speech Ellie gives about the kind of "quality time" she'd like to spend with her family—once she's possessed, and as she's cooking eggs—is one of my favorite moments in recent movie memory. Previously-unknown-to-me model Alyssa Sutherland is capable of being so scary AND such a good comic actor. Overall, this is a really fun franchise that plays with the idea of demonic possession outside of the typical demon box, and has become a real cornerstone in the horror castle.

Nightmare on Elm Street 2: Freddy's Revenge (Jack Sholder, 1985)

This is one of those classic he-wasn't-supposed-to-be-gay movies in which a character is absolutely, unarguably gay. Protagonist Jesse not only fights with Freddy in his dreams, resisting the urge to let the monster in him come out, but he also frequents a gay bar, wrestles with his boyfriends (oops, I mean, friends who are boys) while attempting to rip each others' clothes off, and his body *literally* won't let him kiss a girl. Lots of eighties fun in this one! You can feel a lot of emotion in this movie, and those emotions are heightened by the excellent documentary *Scream, Queen! My Nightmare on Elm Street*, which focuses on lead actor Mark Patton's life on and off screen since the movie came out.

Þorsti (Thirst) **(Steinþór Hróar Steinþórsson & Gaukur Úlfarsson, 2019)**

What a fuuuunnnnn movie! *Þorsti* is an Icelandic gay vampire film, in which a woman overcoming a drug addiction unwittingly befriends a thousand-year-old gay vampire who thirsts for . . . well, blood, like a regular vampire, but also penises, which is not the usual vampiric fare. There are many penises in this movie, lots of people with comically-fake rubber penises getting ripped off, and even a scene in which the vampire eats a penis in a hot dog bun. It's pretty great. The script is a little weak and would have benefitted from not being SO incredibly silly, but a lot of the humor hits home, thanks in part to Jens Jensson's straightlaced portrayal of the detective investigating the crime spree, and Hjörtur Sævar Steinason, the vampire. While this movie won't blow you away, it's worth watching and just a lot of fun, and features an *excellent* electronic soundtrack from David Berndsen.

STRAIGHT FROM OUR BLEEDING HEARTS

We'd Like to Thank a Few People for Helping Us Make This Book

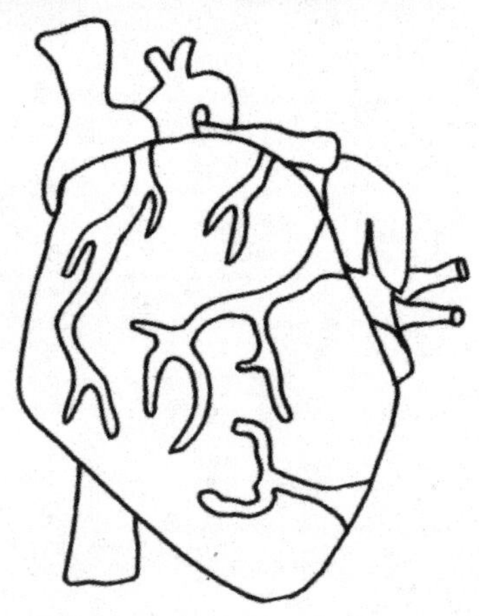

This book would never have been written without the support and encouragement of the many readers of our horror zine series, *Gina & Joe Talk About: Queer Horror*, and its ensuing issues *Halloween Horror*, *Wintry Horrors*, *Queer Horror #2*, and *The Exorcist.* Thanks to all of you who have picked up our zine, posted about it on social media, and written to us with your thoughts about it. Your enthusiasm and camaraderie inspired us to write the book in your hands.

We'd like to extend a big thank you to the booksellers, stores, and distributors who have helped us get our original queer horror zines into the world and into your hands, particularly Joshua at Antiquated Future, Nicole & Nicole at South Street Art Mart, Liz at Vault of Midnight, Steven at Quimby's NYC, Liz at Quimby's CHI, Diana & Breanna at Vault + Vine, and Kali at Pegasus Books. Your distribution was invaluable to us, and we're happy to call you all friends after years of working together.

We'd also like to make sure Joe, Elly, Lex, and everyone else from Microcosm Publishing knows how much we appreciate all they've done for us, and all the guidance they've provided in seeing this book from rough sketch to the beautiful artifact you're holding in your hands.

Gina's Thanks

First and foremost, infinite thanks to my beloved partner Ellen, who for over twenty-five years has read, watched, and listened to horror stories with me (and sometimes even enjoyed them, though *Texas Chainsaw Massacre* and *Hereditary:* never again!). Huge thanks also to Joe, who is not only the best horror partner anyone could ask for but also extremely talented, well-connected, and even-keeled. This book would not have been written without his initiative at every turn, and I feel incredibly lucky to be able to collaborate with him. I would be remiss if I didn't also mention my parents, who never thought I was too young to watch a horror movie or hear about the serial killers in our city's federal prison; and my sister Amy, who revelled in all that early horror with me. Thanks also to the University of Michigan's Institute for the Humanities; their generous fellowship in the summer of 2024 gave me financial and intellectual support for this project. My cohort of fellows and director Peggy McCracken provided me with essential feedback and camaraderie. Special thanks to my friend and colleague Angie Berkley, who was also a member of that cohort and who has always enthusiastically supported Joe's and my zines and read and commented on extra material for me, offering advice that always improved it. Finally, I want to thank the English Department at the University of Michigan for nurturing my interest in horror by giving me the opportunity to teach courses on it, and last but certainly not least, thanks to my students for walking the dark and twisting paths of the genre with me. I would have so much less to say about horror if it weren't for them.

Joe's Thanks

I would like to thank my partner Katie for her unwavering support, her insightful editorial help, and for just being a good person to be with all the time. I'd gush even further, but you're already mentioned in like half of my essays in this book, so I'll leave it at that. I'd also like to thank my friends and family for listening to me talk about horror movies all the time, particularly when I'm stuck on one I didn't like and frankly won't stop talking about *why* I didn't like it. I'd like to thank Gina for being a great friend, an awesome writing partner, and for making the first contact when she bought some zines I'd released of Victorian ghost stories, and for being the one who came up with the idea of doing a queer horror zine together in the first place. She writes warmly of those who helped her come out, and I hope she knows she was one of those people for me. I'd also like to specifically call out MovieJawn, who I've been tabling next to at events since like 2013, and who I really enjoy now writing movie reviews for, even though I enjoy the support and camaraderie of my peers even more, specifically looking at you, Rosalie, Tori, and Matt. Most importantly, and this includes Katie & Gina, I want to thank all of the collaborators and contributors I've had in my zines, records, and cassettes over the years. My work would surely be diminished if not for the support and unbridled creativity of my community of friends, artists, and collaborators. Your work is a constant inspiration to be better in my own.

YOUR BEST GHOULFRIENDS

It's Us, Your Authors

GINA BRANDOLINO

Gina Brandolino is a proud lifetime Midwesterner who lives in Ann Arbor with her partner Ellen. She has a Ph.D. in English literature with a specialization in medieval studies and is a lecturer in the Department of English Language and Literature at the University of Michigan, where she teaches a variety of horror courses and also courses on comics, working class literature, and early English literature. She hosts a regular podcast about teaching with her friend and colleague Angie Berkley called *Behind the Scaffolding*, and in 2023 she hosted a podcast series celebrating the fiftieth anniversary of the classic film *The Exorcist*. You can find both of these wherever you listen to podcasts. Gina curates a horror blog featuring her students' writing about all things spooky; visit it at courseofhorror.wordpress.com. In addition to her writing about horror, she has published articles about medieval literature, higher education, and comics. She prefers fall over spring, ghosts over monsters, Michael over Jason, Ripley over Laurie, and—every single time—the book over the movie.

JOE CARLOUGH

Joe Carlough is a queer DIY enthusiast from Philadelphia. He publishes stuff under the name Displaced Snail. He's a big horror fan and has a Google Sheet on his computer with over five hundred horror movie reviews that he's been keeping since 2017. He also ran the short-lived horror review site Scary Movie Club. He's been making zines since 2007 and has sold something like 45,000 copies of his zines, records, and books as of this publication—all logged on, yes, another spreadsheet. Most recently, he's been learning to master the art of record making using near-antique record lathes, cutting vinyl records one at a time in his home studio. Joe is one half of the art group Consonant Collective with his partner Katie Haegele, and together they release zines, books, and records, give performances, and curate the East Falls Zine Reading Room, a cataloged collection of 1,600 zines. His first book with Microcosm was *The Queer Affirmations Coloring Book*, a book that dissects common idioms and affirmations and rewrites them to put intention back into conversations. If you want to know more about Joe and what he does, you can find him online at displacedsnail.com and consonantcollective.com and on Instagram @displacedsnail. Joe's big on correspondence, so if you write, he'll write back.

QUEER HORROR INDEX

Every Movie, Book, or Other Piece of Media Mentioned in the Book

Books, Novellas, and Short Stories

The Addams Chronicles - Charles Addams

"An Account of Some Strange Disturbances in Aungier Street" - Sheridan Le Fanu

Doctor Faustus - Christopher Marlowe

Danse Macabre - Stephen King

"The Devil and Daniel Webster" - Stephen Vincent Benet

"The Devil and Tom Walker" - Washington Irving

Dracula - Bram Stoker

"The Eyes" - Edith Wharton

Frozen Hell - John W. Campbell

Interview with the Vampire - Anne Rice

It Came from the Closet: Queer Reflections on Horror - ed. Joey Vallese

Men, Women, and Chainsaws: Gender in the Modern Horror Film - Carol Clover

"The Monkey's Paw" - W.W. Jacobs

Moonstone: The Boy Who Never Was - Sjón

My Favorite Thing Is Monsters, Book I - Emil Ferris

My Favorite Thing Is Monsters, Book II - Emil Ferris

The Queer Affirmations Coloring Book - Joe Carlough, Ally Shwed

The Shining - Stephen King

Spiritbox - Katie Haegele

Strange Case of Dr. Jekyll and Mr. Hyde - Robert Louis Stevenson

The Turn of the Screw - Henry James

The Vampire Chronicles - Anne Rice

The Vanishing Hitchhiker: American Urban Legends and Their Meanings - Jan Harold Brunvand

Who Goes There? - John W. Campbell

Movies

30 Days of Night (2007)

Adam (1983)

The Addams Family (1991)

Alien (1979)

Alien³ (1992)

Alien Resurrection (1997)

Aliens (1986)

Alone with You (2021)

Amityville Horror (1979)

Amityville Horror: It's About Time (1992)

Amityville Horror 4: The Evil Escapes (1989)

Army of Darkness (1992)

The Babadook (2014)

The Bad Seed (2018)

The Bare-Breasted Countess (1973)

The Beach House (2019)

Black Christmas (1974)

Black Swan (2010)

The Blackcoat's Daughter (2015)

The Breakfast Club (1985)

Butcher, Baker, Nightmare Maker (1981)

Chopping Mall (1986)

The Cold (aka *The Game*) (1984)

Cold Skin (2017)

Crawl (2019)

Crimson Peak (2015)

Crocodile Dundee (1986)

The Dark and the Wicked (2020)

The Dark Crystal (1982)

Daughters of Darkness (1971)

Demons (1985)

Devil's Advocate (1997)

The Devil Inside (2012)

Erotikill (1973)

Event Horizon (1997)

Evil Dead (2013)

The Evil Dead (1981)

The Evil Dead II (1987)

Evil Dead Rise (2023)

Exorcism: The Possession of Gail Bowers (2006)

The Exorcism of Emily Rose (2005)

The Exorcist (1973)

Fatal Vision (1984)

Female Vampire (1973)

Ferris Bueller's Day Off (1986)

The Fog (1980)

Get Out (2017)

Ghostwatch (1992)

Grey Gardens (1975)

Gypsy 83 (2001)

Halloween (1978)

Halloween II (1981)

Halloween III (1982)

The Haunting (1963)

Hell House LLC (2015)

Hereditary (2018)

House on Haunted Hill (1959)

Horror Express (1972)

I Saw the TV Glow (2024)

It Follows (2014)

The Jessica Cabin (2023)

Jumping Jack Flash (1986)

Lamb (2021)

The Last Exorcism (2010)

Last House on the Left (1972)

Lizzie (2018)

Let the Right One In (2008)

Love Lies Bleeding (2024)

Mega Python vs. Gatoroid (2011)

Mega Shark vs. Giant Octopus (2009)

Mega Shark vs. Mecha Shark (2014)

The Midnight Swim (2014)

Mimic (1997)

Mommie Dearest (1981)

The Monster Club (1981)

Near Dark (1987)

Night of the Comet (1984)

Night of the Demons (1988)

Night of the Living Dead (1968)

Nightmare on Elm Street (1984)

Nightmare on Elm Street 2: Freddy's Revenge (1985)

Old Dark House (1932)

Phantom of the Mall: Eric's Revenge (1989)

Poltergeist (1982)

Poltergeist II (1986)

Popcorn (1991)

The Possession (2012)

The Possession of Hannah Grace (2018)

Pretty in Pink (1986)

Prom Night 2: Hello Mary Lou (1987)

Relic (1997)

Rift (2017)

The Ring (2002)

Saint Maud (2019)

Scream, Queen! My Nightmare on Elm Street (2019)

Screams of a Winter Night (1979)

Sea Fever (2019)

The Shape of Water (2017)

The Shining (1980)

The Silence of the Lambs (1991)

Sisters of Death (1977)

Sleepaway Camp (1983)

Sorority Row (2009)

Spiral (2019)

Splice (2009)

The Strings (2020)

Sunset Boulevard (1950)

The Texas Chainsaw Massacre (1974)

The Thing (1982)

The Thing (2011)

The Thing from Another World (1951)

Þorsti (*Thirst*) (2019)

Top Gun (1986)

Trick r' Treat (2007)

The Village of the Damned (1960)

We're All Going to the World's Fair (2021)

Wendigo (2001)

Wham Bam Thank You Spaceman (1975)

What Keeps You Alive (2018)

The VVitch (2015)

Witchboard (1986)

WNUF Halloween Special (2013)

TV Shows

The Addams Family

Ash vs. Evil Dead

The Boulet Brothers' Dragula

Creepshow

The Exorcist

Ghost Adventures

Ghost Hunters

Good Times

The Jeffersons

Laverne and Shirley

Living for the Dead

Paranormal Caught on Camera

Paranormal State

Queer Eye

RuPaul's Drag Race

Seinfeld

Survivor

True Blood

Essays

"My Words to Victor Frankenstein above the Village of Chamounix: Performing Transgender Rage" - Susan Stryker

"There's Something Inside of Me: Coming Out as a Gay Horror Fan" - Louis Pietzman

Zines

Salvation! - Rose Glass

Weird NJ

Games

Animal Crossing: New Horizons

Castlevania

Dungeons & Dragons

Five Nights at Freddy's

The Legend of Zelda

Skyrim

Stardew Valley

Music

"The Devil Went down to Georgia" - Charlie Daniels Band

"These Lights" - The Forecast

Bauhaus

Podcasts

Taking on the Devil: Celebrating 50 Years of The Exorcist

Poems

"Goblin Market" - Christina Rossetti

Theater

Phantom of the Opera

Swan Lake